Why I Jumped

Why I Jumped

*My True Story of Postpartum Depression,
Dramatic Rescue & Return to Hope*

Tina Zahn
with Wanda Dyson

Revell
Grand Rapids, Michigan

Published by Fleming H. Revell
a division of Baker Publishing Group
P.O. Box 6287, Grand Rapids, MI 49516-6287

Printed in the United States of America

Library of Congress Cataloging-in-Publication Data is on file at the Library of Congress, Washington, D.C.

ISBN 10: 0-8007-1891-7
ISBN 978-0-8007-1891-6
ISBN International 10: 0-8007-1900-X
ISBN International 978-0-8007-1900-5

Unless otherwise indicated, Scripture is taken from the HOLY BIBLE, NEW INTERNA-TIONAL VERSION®. NIV®. Copyright © 1973, 1978, 1984 by International Bible Society. Used by permission of Zondervan. All rights reserved.

Published in association with the literary agency of WordServe Literary Group, Ltd., 10152 S. Knoll Circle, Highlands Ranch, CO 80130.

Interior design by Brian Brunsting

This book is dedicated to the "power of community"—to all of you who prayed for and encouraged me and my family in the darkest hours. Please hold Daniel and me accountable for building well on the foundation you laid.

And to my daughter, Sarah, who loved me through the writing of this book with her warm hugs, brilliant smile, and unique and touching artwork.

To Noah, who cheerfully went off to Marcia's to play so Mommy could work, and then greeted me with those big loving smiles when it was time to come home.

And to my husband, Daniel, for being my rock.

Tina Zahn

To Christi for being there. To my daughter, Jayme, for taking the backseat while Mommy worked and never complaining about it. And to Greg and Becky Johnson for all they did to make this possible.

Wanda Dyson

Contents

"For I know the plans I have for you," declares the LORD, "plans to prosper you and not to harm you, plans to give you hope and a future."

Jeremiah 29:11

And we know that in all things God works for the good of those who love him, who have been called according to his purpose.

Romans 8:28

Prologue

July 19, 2004
Green Bay, Wisconsin

Nine-one-one. What is your emergency?"

Tucking the cell phone under his chin, Daniel Zahn whipped the steering wheel to the left, making a sharp turn, cutting off the highway and across the median. His Durango bounced, skidding across the grass as he accelerated. "My wife. She's going to jump!"

"I'm sorry, sir. Your wife is going to jump what?"

"The Tower Drive Bridge. She's going to jump off the bridge!" His tires caught pavement, the car fishtailing a bit before lurching forward, nearly knocking his cell phone off his shoulder. He grabbed it. "You have to stop her!"

"Can you tell me where you are, sir?"

Frustration and rising panic surged through Daniel as he watched his wife's car up ahead of him weave through the traffic and disappear. "On 29 . . . a couple miles east of Pack-erland. She's heading for 41."

"And where are you, sir?"

"Westbound on . . ." *No, that wasn't right. He'd made a U-turn after spotting Tina's car and was now racing to catch up with her.* "*East*bound on 29. I'm in a Durango. She's driving a white Oldsmobile Aurora."

"Can you see her?"

"No . . . Yes! She's getting in the left-turn lane at Packerland. I think she may be heading home." Relief rushed over him, nearly snatching his breath away, but it was short-lived. He watched in disbelief as Tina whipped her car around waiting traffic and shot through the intersection.

"No! She didn't turn! She didn't turn! She's going for the bridge!"

Parked in a vacant grocery store lot, Sergeant Bill Morgan kept half an ear on the radio as he filled out paperwork. Suddenly he heard dispatch call him.

"Headquarters, four-Ida, Lincoln one-ninety-two."

Grabbing the mic, he checked in. "Four-Ida."

Immediately he heard Deputy Bill Roche check in as well. "One-ninety-two."

"10-4, Ida. We have a 98 Olds Aurora, white. There is a suicidal female in the vehicle going ninety miles per hour at this time on 29 eastbound. Severely depressed. Subject's husband is on the line. She's coming up on Packerland."

Thirty-odd years of training kicked in as Sergeant Morgan turned his car onto Highway 29, coaching his deputies into their places like football players, well-trained team members knowing their part of the drill and carrying it out like the pros they were. He'd known of others who had jumped from that bridge and didn't survive. There was no way he was going to let the Fox River claim another victim if he could help it.

Just as he pulled his squad car up on the ramp to 41 to watch for the white Oldsmobile, an unmarked state trooper's car went screaming past, lights flashing and sirens blaring. He grabbed his mic as his foot hit the accelerator. "I think her car just went by. Is someone behind her in an unmarked squad car?"

"10-4, Ida. State car is behind her. She's passing cars on the shoulder."

"I'm right behind him." Morgan glanced down at his speedometer as he hit his siren. Seventy miles per hour and climbing. Eighty. Ninety. And still he couldn't catch up. And the ramp for Highway 43 was coming up fast. Hitting his brakes, he swung over into the right lane.

Suddenly dispatch barked into the radio. "State Police Officer Boldt is right behind her, but she isn't pulling over. She's increased speed. All units be advised. She is heading for the bridge."

The dump truck in front of Morgan slowed down for the treacherous S-turn on the exit ramp, either ignoring or unable to hear the sirens right behind him. Morgan moved a little to the left, hoping to get the truck driver's attention, but the effort was wasted. The truck merely slowed into the turn, leaving no room for Morgan to slide past him.

Slamming his hand on the steering wheel, he eased back to

wait for his chance to get around the dump truck. He could only pray there was enough time. Once he hit the bottom of the ramp, it would be just over a mile to the bridge.

Seconds felt like minutes. As he monitored his deputies, received updates on the suicidal woman, and impatiently followed the dump truck, Bill Morgan felt his heart pounding into overdrive.

When they reached the bottom of the ramp, Bill glanced in his mirrors, saw the opening, and shot out onto Highway 43. Up ahead he could see Boldt's lights flashing. He pressed down on the accelerator, taking the squad car to the limit. Ninety. One hundred. One-ten. One-twenty.

He hit the bottom of the bridge and saw the state police car skid to a stop at the top of the bridge. "No. No. No." He glanced in his rearview mirror and saw another car—lights flashing—right on his tail.

He grabbed his mic. "We're on the bridge."

Slamming on the brakes, he skidded to a stop next to Boldt's car. There was no sign of the woman. And no sign of Trooper Boldt. His heart fell, and he reported back to dispatch. "She jumped!"

Preface

A Few Thoughts . . .

If you're not prepared, the drama of this book could wear you out. It's my real-life drama, dealing with postpartum depression (PPD) and the traumas I have endured throughout my life.

Many women who suffer from postpartum depression get over it quickly. They had a good childhood and no other psychological issues, and not long after giving birth, the chemical imbalance they experienced returns to normal. End of story. But if there are other emotional traumas that haven't been dealt with, the postpartum trigger can drop a huge emotional bomb into a woman's life.

I'm the first to admit that some aspects of my story are extreme. I didn't just have PPD. I had PPD as well as long-term sexual abuse by someone I trusted. I didn't experience only PPD and sexual abuse, but my mother rejected me when she discovered the abuse. I didn't experience only the PPD, the sexual abuse, and the rejection, but the residual effects of these things led to my making bad decisions, which in turn produced other hurtful events. It was a never-ending cycle that led me to the bridge that morning.

I'm not writing this book so that people will feel sorry for me. Rather, I want this book to give someone else hope, the hope that she can be a survivor and start living a happy and whole life. And while this book will firmly address the important issue of PPD, my problems were much bigger than that. They stemmed from childhood trauma, emotional triggers, unresolved pain, abandonment, marital dilemmas, and faith trials. But my story is also about many great friends, successes, setbacks, and finally a road filled with hope. My story is about a lifetime packaged with pain, and how through the gift of friendship, a strong measure of faith, a loving spouse, and some good medications, I have progressed from wanting to end it all to having much more to look forward to than I could ever have imagined.

What I want to say is this: if I can make it through all of the traumas I've gone through, you or your loved one can too!

It wasn't easy. It didn't happen overnight. But the process was worth it, every painful step. And while I know that I am not yet 100 percent out of the woods emotionally, I also know that few people are. We all carry baggage that affects us in our adult years.

I've changed the names of many people in this book to protect their privacy. I've tried to tell my story to the best of my ability and recollection. For parts of the story, I've had to rely on others to fill in the gaps of my memory or for information I didn't know at the time the events were happening. For instance, when you read my account of the jump later in the book, I obviously didn't know the officers' names at the time they were pursuing me, but it is easier to tell the story now by identifying them by name.

If you're experiencing any kind of abuse or depression, it is essential for you to seek professional advice, whether medical, psychological, or legal. Nothing in this book is intended to provide specific advice for your situation. It is simply a telling of my own story.

I'm going to start where my story begins. And if you'll stay with me, you'll see how hope begins and how happy endings are possible. And I think you'll see that God did a miracle in me and in my family.

Because of the grip of a caring and brave policeman, I've been given a second chance at life. And because of that, I get to experience the joy of two precious children, my husband, and my friends, joy that I would have missed out on had I been successful in jumping two hundred feet to my death.

You know some of the ending—I'm still here! But the story has a beginning, an all too familiar beginning. So let's start there, just a few months after my fifth birthday. I had been excited about starting school, but that excitement was wiped

out, and each day at school became little more than a temporary reprieve from my suffering. When I was only five, all my
joy, innocence, and naïveté were shattered, and life became a
living nightmare.

chapter one

Little Girl Lost

August 1973
Ashwaubenon, Wisconsin

Whitney, take Kyle outside and play, but you stay in the yard. You hear me?" My father yelled the directions to my younger sister.

I was lying on the floor with a puzzle, engrossed in the delight of the picture falling into place. Just a few more pieces and I'd be done. I had turned five years old in April and my mom and dad had given me the puzzle for my birthday. It was a great puzzle, so I dawdled for a few more minutes. I didn't want to go outside with Kyle and Whitney; I wanted to finish my puzzle, but as Whitney passed me, holding Kyle's hand, I stood up and followed them to the back door.

"Not you, Tina. You stay here," Dad said.

Whitney, younger than me by a year, gave me a smirk. She thought I was in trouble. But I hadn't done anything; at least, not that I could remember.

"Tina! Get downstairs. Now!"

There was something in my dad's voice that made everything in me go very, very still. It was more than a tone that brooked no argument—he always had that—but this was something deeper and far more intimidating. Slowly I walked over to the basement steps. I hated going down into that basement. There were spiders down there.

"Why?"

He grabbed my arm and jerked me forward. "Don't ask me stupid questions. Just do what I tell you."

Mom was at work, so there would be no help from her, although it was rare that she would challenge Dad about anything he chose to do. My mind raced with questions. What had I done to make him mad? Why did I have to go to the basement? Maybe someone had spilled laundry detergent on the floor and I was going to get punished for it.

The basement was cool and damp, the concrete blocks marked in some places by water stains and mold. Old boxes were stacked in a corner, holding belongings that the family no longer used. My sled hung from nails in the exposed beams overhead, along with ice skates, wire, fishing poles, and rope. The washing machine stood silent under the single bulb that hung from the ceiling and gave a little light to the dreary basement. The two well windows let in precious little sun.

"Daddy?" We reached the bottom of the steps and he took

my arm again, leading me back around under the stairs to the desk he had set up. My mother had wondered why he wanted to set up a small office down in the basement—it was so dank and dark—but he insisted he needed a quiet place to work.

Dad sat down in his chair and lifted me up onto his lap. "It's okay, honey. I'm not mad at you."

"You're not?"

He stroked my hair, my arm, and my back, but rather than bringing me comfort, his attention confused me. There was tension in him that I could associate only with his anger, and yet he was smiling and softening his voice in a way that confirmed his words. So why didn't I feel better?

"No, honey. I love you. You know that. I just want to show you how much I love you. How much you mean to me. You love me, don't you, Tina?"

"Yes, Daddy."

"Of course you do, and I want to show you how to prove to me that you love me."

I began to shake, but I wasn't cold. It didn't make sense to me. It felt like the walls were slowly closing in on me. Then the spiders would be closer. The dank, moldy smell made the space seem even smaller, tighter, more frightening.

"I'm going to teach you how to love me. I'm going to show you how to please me. But this is going to be our little secret, okay? We're not going to tell anyone, understand?"

I shook my head. I didn't understand at all.

He blew out this big heavy sigh as his hands roamed, making

me squirm, but he didn't seem to mind the squirming at all. "It'll be good, Tina. You'll see. You'll love it."

But I didn't love it at all. I hated it. I hated the way he breathed. I hated the way he held me down. I hated the smells. I hated feeling helpless. And most of all, I hated the pain.

I didn't want to think about my dad or what he was doing to me or the helplessness I felt or the screams that were lodged in my throat. I turned my thoughts outward, trying to concentrate on happy thoughts. Whitney on the swing in the backyard. Kyle pushing her higher and higher. My mom working over at Kmart, and the candy she might bring home after work. My grandparents up in Michigan, and the delightful smells that always greeted me when I went there to visit. The new baby that was coming.

I thought about the firehouse across the street, and all my happy thoughts fled. All this time it had represented safety to me. If anything happened, help was just across the street. But no help was coming. How foolish I had been. Safety was an illusion.

I had no idea how to deal with the helplessness I felt or the pain. My dad had sworn me to secrecy. No one could ever know. Dad hadn't actually threatened me, but the threat was there, verbalized or not. If I told anyone, the family would be ripped apart, and I didn't know what would happen to me.

For weeks my helplessness haunted every waking thought. It was like being trapped in a maze with no way out. But there was one shining light in my week—Sunday morning. My parents were both raised Catholic, but my mom was the only one who faithfully went to mass on Sunday morning. She would usually take me with her, leaving my siblings home with Dad. In the past it was just something we did together, my mom and I, but now those Sunday mornings became one of those precious times when I felt free from my dad, when I knew he couldn't get to me.

Nativity Church was the largest Catholic church in the Green Bay area. Mom always sat on the right-hand side, in the same pew, where each time you looked up from your prayers you were staring into the face of Mary. This was a source of conflict for me. My great-grandmother was a Lutheran, and she kept telling me that praying to Mary was wrong—that I was supposed to pray to Jesus.

But I had bigger conflicts now than whether or not to pray to Mary, so I prayed my little heart out that God would do something, anything, to change the circumstances of my life.

"Are you still interested in joining the Brownies?" Mom asked me as she lowered the kneeling bench.

I glanced at her as we both knelt. "Yes!" I told her with a big smile. "I can?"

"I talked it over with your dad and he said you can join."

At the mention of my dad, my smile faded as fast as my happiness. The darkness dropped down over me as I stared down at my hands, clasped tightly in front of me. She didn't know. Couldn't know. I was trapped in a nightmare that had no end. Sometimes I would go to school with terrific stomachaches, and my mother would have to come and take me home, but she had no idea what was causing the problem.

Each time my dad headed for the basement door and looked at me, everything in me would freeze in dread and fear. Every time my mom left for work, the helplessness would begin to overwhelm me. He'd touch me and I would want to scream but couldn't. He'd take my hand and I'd want to run away but couldn't. He would tell me what he wanted and I could only comply.

Mom put her hand on my shoulder. "Pray."

"Yes, Mommy." I looked around at the congregation as everyone stared forward, praying silently.

Did anyone suspect what was going on inside my house? I don't think so. My dad went to great lengths to make sure the community thought we were the perfect family. But behind closed doors, the house was submerged in tension, anger, violence, and pain—secrets that had to be kept no matter what.

August 1974
Menominee, Michigan

"Grandma!" I came running into the kitchen, the screen door slapping closed behind me as I skidded barefoot across the old linoleum floor. "Look what I got!"

I held out two apples. "See?"

She was a small woman and she didn't talk much, but for the past week she had been a huge enclave of security and peace for me. I was safe here. I could run all day without fear of hearing *him* call my name. I could laugh without fear of attracting his attention. I could run through the house with a sense of freedom I hadn't known for a year.

"Nice," Grandma replied as she measured some flour into a bowl, barely glancing at the apples.

"Where's Grandpa?"

She nodded her head toward the back of the house. "Garage."

I found him under the hood of his truck, tinkering with something. "Grandpa! I'm picking apples!"

He lifted his head, pushing back his cap. "Well, so you are. And aren't those fine ones too."

Up on tiptoe I tried to look over the fender and down into the engine of Grandpa's truck. "Whatcha doin'?"

"Timing's off. Just adjusting it."

"Can I help?"

He set the timing light down on the fender and ruffled my hair. "I have a better idea. Why don't we go find some more apples? I'll bet we can convince your grandma to make us a cobbler or a pie."

"I know where they are!"

Adjusting his ball cap, he gave me one of those smiles that always warmed me right down to my toes. Everything was contained in that smile—love, acceptance, affection, approval.

After grabbing a deep basket from the back porch, the two of us headed off to the small orchard behind the house. There were twelve apple trees, all heavy with fruit.

As we walked hand in hand to the orchard, I lifted my face to the sun. It was wonderful, so bright and warm—everything that the basement at home was not. I wanted to live in the sunshine all the time.

"Here they are, Grandpa!" I skipped up to the trees, spinning around in a circle, laughing as it made me a little dizzy.

"Don't hurt yourself, girl." But his warning was tempered by the laughter in his voice.

I stopped and grinned at him as the world went a little topsy-turvy. My grandfather sold and repaired farm machinery and worked very hard. He was usually really tired when he got home, but he always had a smile and a hug for me.

"Up you go, girl." He bent over so that I could climb up on his shoulders and from there, pick the fruit off the limbs rather than picking up dropped apples off the ground.

As I picked each apple, I'd hand it down to him and he'd drop it in the basket. For a few minutes, neither of us spoke. Words weren't necessary. He had one hand firmly on my thigh to keep me from falling if I lost my balance, and he was the only man who could touch my leg without arousing terror. His grip on my leg brought comfort and security, not the cold sweat of fear.

"Now this is a beauty," he said, holding out a McIntosh apple I had picked. "Good work."

Pleasure rolled through me, inspiring me to work even harder, picking the best, ripest, juiciest apples as fast as I could. I had found one experience in my life that made me feel really good—pleasing other people. As long as I could please them, maybe they wouldn't see the ugliness that I felt loomed inside of me.

Tina gives her dog, Jock, a bath.

Tina and Kyle playing croquet in Michigan.

How I loved visiting my grandparents' house! What child could resist these wonderful, loving people? Every day was an adventure that brought hugs and kisses and smiles. There was no tension in the air, no secrets in the basement, just pure, simple pleasure.

The apple pie was wonderful—still warm from the oven when Grandma served it for dinner. She let me whip fresh cream into cold clouds of fluff, and my mouth watered as I watched her put a generous dollop on my pie. I had just finished scraping the last of the cream off my plate when I heard a car pull in. I didn't think much of it until I heard my mother's voice at the front door.

"Hello?"

My grandmother stood up, gathering the dinner dishes. "We're in the kitchen, dear."

I felt as though someone had taken me from my warm perch on the edge of paradise and thrown me into an icy lake. My heart beat a rhythm of dread in my small chest. "Why are you here, Momma?"

She brushed my hair back off my shoulders, frowning at the tangles in it. "I came to pick you up and take you home."

"I don't wanna go home."

Her frown deepened. "Don't start this again, Tina. We go through this every time you come to stay here. Now your visit is over. School will be starting soon."

Tears began to stream down my face. "I don't wanna go back there. Can't I just live with Grandma and Grandpa?"

I could see the anger in her eyes, but I didn't care. I didn't want to leave. I didn't want to go back there to *him.*

My mother stiffened. "No, you can't stay. Now, go get your stuff. I need to get back on the road. We have a long drive ahead of us."

Grandma gave me a warm, reassuring smile, but it didn't thaw the cold fear. "You'll come back to visit again, sweetheart. Now mind your mother and go get your clothes."

I couldn't do it. I knew I'd just get in more trouble, but I had to try. I just had to.

"No! I don't want to leave. You can't make me!"

My mother took my arm and pulled me toward her. "I can and I will. Now mind me or it will get worse for you."

The problem was that I knew it was going to get worse if I

did mind her. "Don't make me go, please." I ran to my grandfather and wrapped my arms around his neck, clinging as hard as I could.

My mother wasn't going to relent. "I don't have time for this. Now go pack."

Sobbing in my grandfather's arms, I shook my head.

My grandfather slowly eased my arms from around his neck. "What's wrong, Tina?"

I couldn't tell him. I couldn't tell anyone. Hanging my head, I continued to sob. My mother placed her hands on my shoulders and turned me toward the doorway. "Go pack, young lady. Now."

Dragging my feet, I made my way into the bedroom and slowly tossed all my clothes into my suitcase. There would be no miracle, no way of escape. When we got back home, *he* would be waiting, and soon I would be struggling with my secret pain and shame.

As we drove toward Green Bay, the miles of orchards and small towns didn't distract me from the fear in the pit of my stomach. I wanted desperately to tell my mom about what Daddy was doing to me, but I was afraid. If she tried to tell Daddy to stop, he might hit her again—as he had many times before when she disagreed with him. Then there was the other possibility—if she thought Daddy was right, she would be angry with me and maybe stop loving me, and he might hurt me even more.

"I have good news for you." Mom's voice interrupted my thoughts.

I continued to stare out the window at the landscape—the

endlessly green forests and occasional farms, the cattle and the cornfields. "What good news?"

"Well, two things actually. The first is I heard from your Brownie leader."

That got my attention and I turned to look at her. She kept her eyes on the road as she talked. "You sold the most cookies this year and you're getting a trophy."

"I am?" My heart skipped a beat. I'd won. All that hard work had paid off. Mom had helped me, of course, but I'd won. "When do I get my trophy?"

"At the next meeting."

Grinning, I stared out the front windshield, no longer seeing the road. I was thinking about standing up and receiving my trophy and how everyone would envy me. How my mom would smile and hug me and be so proud of me. I would please her, and this brought its own pleasure to me.

"I also wanted to tell you that your dad and I found a new house," she said, "and we're moving next month."

"Moving?"

There was a rush of emotion at that news. We would move and then I wouldn't have to go down into that basement ever again.

Mom cleared her throat. "We're moving up to Shawano. We found a lovely house right on the river."

"Does it have a basement?"

She gave me a strange look, but I didn't expect her to understand my question. How could she?

"Not really. Not a basement like we have now. The lower

level has these big windows that look out over the river. And there are two bedrooms down there."

A shiver went down my spine and I clenched my hands.

"Unfortunately, you have to go through one bedroom to get to the second, but I think we'll put your brother in the first bedroom and you and your sisters can share the other."

Relief flooded through me, all warm and tingly. Maybe, just maybe, things would change. I'd have Whitney and Nadine, my baby sister, as protection and my brother too. If *he* couldn't get to me, maybe it would stop. With the fear subsiding, other questions formed. "Why are we moving?"

"Do you remember Pastor Tim?"

I nodded. Pastor Tim was the pastor of a Lutheran church up in Shawano, and even though my mom and dad were Catholic, Daddy was fond of Pastor Tim.

"Daddy wants to start attending Pastor Tim's church. Actually he wants the whole family to attend, so we're moving up there to be close to the church." She stopped for a red light, flashing me a weak smile.

"So we're not going to be Catholic anymore?"

She merely shook her head. I guess she wasn't altogether happy about any of this, but I thought it was fine. We would be Lutheran just like my great-grandmother.

With each mile that passed, we edged closer to home and the anxiety within me rose. If my mom noticed, she didn't comment on it. By the time we walked through the front door, I felt like a frightened rabbit about to be cornered by a fox. My heart pounded, my hands were moist and shaking. I couldn't bring myself to look my dad in the eye as I hurried through the living room and into my bedroom, shutting the door behind me as tightly as possible.

After unpacking, I sat on the edge of my bed. How soon would we be moving? How soon would this nightmare end?

It wasn't ending anytime soon. I found that out the next day when Daddy called me down into the basement again. I don't think he was too happy about not having me around for a week because everything changed. Now, not only did he want to do unspeakable things to me, he also expected me to learn how to do horrid things to him.

I began to count the days until we moved.

It proved to be only a matter of weeks before we were all moved into our new home. It was a pretty, two-story brick home with blue shutters, sitting on the Wolf River, a beautiful waterway filled with trout, walleyes, and brightly colored stones. There were only four houses on the street, all overlooking the river, and only two of them had year-round tenants. The other two were occupied by their owners only during the summer.

The lower level was indeed nothing like the basement of my nightmares. Big bay windows overlooked the river, letting in plenty of light and making the area more like any first floor of a home. My brother's room was small and had no windows, but he didn't seem to mind. On the other side of his room was the room I was to share with my sisters. As I stood there and looked out the window, my first thought was that I would be safe here. How could my father sneak through Kyle's room and into my room without risking waking up either my brother or sisters?

"Tina!" my brother called out to me. "Come see this."

I found him at the patio door that led to the backyard. "What?"

He glanced around to make sure no one was looking and jerked his head to indicate he wanted me to follow him.

We ran down to the edge of the river, which was surprisingly shallow at the bank. Kyle pointed down as he kicked off his sandals and waded in. "Can you believe it?"

Stones, brightly colored stones of every shape and size. They were beautiful. I couldn't resist. Looking over my shoulder to make sure my parents weren't watching, I tossed off my flip-flops and waded in to collect the prettiest of the stones.

Every once in a while, Kyle would hold up a particularly nice one and grin at me. Then a man in a canoe paddled by, and we stood there in awe and watched him glide past us. When he waved at us, we waved back with exuberance.

I was so happy, I giggled. It was over. The pain, the hopelessness, the fear. No more.

And then suddenly *he* was there, frowning at us with a look in his eye that had Kyle and me scrambling for the bank. "Are the two of you finished unpacking the boxes in your rooms?"

Kyle shook his head. I dropped my head and stared at my feet, afraid to meet his eyes.

"Then I suggest the two of you get back in that house and finish what you were told to do. And if I catch you out here again before it's all done, you won't be getting near this water for two weeks. Do you understand me?"

We both murmured "yes" and then ran for the house. But even getting into trouble couldn't dampen my happiness.

November 1975

Thanksgiving was just a few weeks away, and already my mom and I had decorated the house with colorful turkeys, pilgrim hats, and cornucopias. My grandparents were coming down from Michigan, we'd be out of school for a long weekend, and then the Christmas season would officially start.

As we sat at the dinner table eating meat loaf and mashed potatoes, my parents talked about those grownup topics that kids usually ignore while kicking each other under the table, pitching peas at each other when no one is looking, and making faces to try to get someone else in trouble.

"I don't know why they can't find a cleaning company," Dad said with a frustrated sigh, "but until they do, we're all responsible for cleaning our own offices."

I'm not sure what made me suddenly start paying attention. Maybe it was a familiar tone in Dad's voice or something in his eyes when he looked over at me or just a sense that something wasn't the way it was supposed to be. Ignoring Whitney's attempts to sneak her vegetables onto my plate, I turned my attention to my parents' conversation. My dad had changed jobs and was now working at a different office. I thought he really liked his new job, so I wasn't quite sure why he was complaining.

Or maybe something about the complaint didn't ring true to me.

My mom didn't seem to notice. "Well, you know I'd help you if it was any other day, but I clean the house on Saturdays. I don't have time to do your office as well."

Daddy wiped his mouth with the napkin, tossed it down, and pushed his plate aside. "I could just take Tina and let her clean while I finish up some accounts I need to update by Monday morning. There's just some dusting, light vacuuming, cleaning the coffeepots, and maybe emptying the trash can. She's old enough to handle stuff like that."

Mom glanced over at me and then nodded. "Sure she could. And you'd like to help your daddy out, wouldn't you, Tina?"

I felt my head move up and down slowly, giving her the answer she wanted while my mind was racing. Why did I feel so icky inside? I tried to tell myself that I was just going to do a little cleaning. Nothing to be afraid of, right? After all, it had been nearly two months since Daddy had hurt me.

But the next morning, when we arrived at my daddy's office, my worst fears were realized. The nightmare was starting all over again. As soon as we got inside the office and he shut the door, I jumped, and my heart became lodged somewhere in my throat.

"Come here, Tina." He sat down behind his desk and held out his arms.

Emotions rolled through me, so strong I didn't know what to do with them. All I could do was obey robotically as my mind began to fracture and slip away from what was happening to me. In my head I went off to play somewhere in another reality, while a nightmare of epic proportions was happening to my physical body. It was the only way I could make sense of my shattered world.

Suddenly there was a knock at the door. Daddy shoved me under his desk, locking me in place with his knees as he scooted up to the desk. The door opened and one of Daddy's co-workers came in.

"What are you doing here on a Saturday? I thought I was the only one that couldn't stay away from all this fun."

Daddy laughed—a low rumble in his throat that made him tighten his hold on me. I knew what he was telling me. Silence.

"Just had some files I needed to update before Monday. Wife is running errands so figured this was as good a time as any. You ready for Monday's meeting?"

"Yeah. My wife is having one of those women things. Tupperware Party or something. So I'm just hiding out until it's over."

Daddy laughed again. "Women and their excuses to get together. They will go to any lengths, won't they? A party to buy and sell plastic containers for leftovers. I mean, could it get any sillier?"

The man chuckled. "Do you see us men having little parties to buy and sell oil filters?"

"That's why they call them the weaker sex."

Both men laughed and then the door closed again. Daddy's knees relaxed their hold on me.

"That was close," he muttered as he pushed back from the desk. "Next time, we lock the door."

Next time?

It came to me like a flash of white-hot lightning. He was never going to stop. It was never going to end. There was no escape. The best I could hope for were brief times of relief when I could wade in the river, play with my friends at recess, and visit my grandparents.

I felt something deep inside give up fighting and die as my daddy continued to touch me. I looked over at the office door. It was closed, shutting me out from the world. No one would ever know. No one could ever save me. There would always be a closed door between the world and me.

Then something I had heard at church popped into my mind. God can do anything. I closed my eyes. *God, make him stop. Please, make him stop.*

It was merely a whisper of a prayer deep in my heart, but it was the only hope I had left.

October 1976

After nearly two years at the house on Wolf River, we were moving again. My mom said the landlord was being unreasonable. Daddy said that it was time to have their own home. They both said the new house would be closer to the church we were now attending.

Along with my brother and sister, I had been enrolled at

Divine Savior's Christian Day School. For a few weeks after, hope had moved into the house, permeating everyone, but it soon became clear that Dad's increased church attendance wasn't going to make much difference within the walls of our home. Daddy was still hurting me. He had started beating my brother, and he and my mother fought as much as ever, sometimes escalating into violence.

One evening hearing Mom's scream, Kyle and I jumped to our feet, abandoning our homework. Nadine, now just three years old, started crying in front of the television. Leaving her to cry, Kyle and I raced from the living room to the kitchen. Mom was on the floor, and Daddy was sitting on her, punching her in the face.

Kyle started screaming, "Stop it! Stop it!" and tried to grab Daddy's arm. Daddy flung him off and my brother hit the floor.

I jumped on Daddy's back, screaming for him to leave my mom alone, but he flung me off easily.

Kyle reached for the phone. "Mommy! I'll call the police!"

Those were the magic words. As if propelled by a spring, he jumped off Mom and took a step toward my brother and me, temper snapping like severed electrical wires, lips curled back in a sneering growl. "Don't you even think of picking up that phone, you hear me?"

Kyle and I knew better than to say a word. I merely looked down at Mom, who was struggling to sit up, wiping the blood from her face. "Go back to your rooms, kids. Now," she said.

Dismissed, Kyle and I picked up our schoolbooks and went

to our rooms. Whitney was seven years old at this time, and I found her sitting in the corner with her thumb in her mouth, clutching her blankie and crying. I sat down and put my arms around her. "Don't cry, Whitney. It will be okay. Kyle and I will take care of you."

I held her thin, trembling body as she cried out her pain and fear, burying her face in my shoulder. I wanted to sob too but knew I needed to hold it together for my sister's sake.

In our home violence erupted frequently without warning and, just as often, without cause. When Daddy started going to church and reading his Bible, I thought the daily horrors would stop. I was wrong.

Whitney sniffed, lifting her head and swiping at her tears. "Maybe things will be better at the new house," she whispered.

I no longer had the capacity to hope that changing locations would bring a better life.

chapter two

Lies, Secrets,
and Broken Dreams

My mom and I stepped into my grandparents' house and, for the first time in my life, the place didn't reach out and embrace me with its usual warmth. There was a heaviness in the house that permeated everything and everyone. Uncle Richie stood in the doorway to the kitchen, eyes red, staring as if he'd never seen us before. He was a stocky man, standing just about six feet tall with auburn hair.

Grandma slowly brushed past him and embraced my mom. "Go on in. He's waiting for you."

My mom put her hand on my shoulder. "Stay here." When she disappeared down the hall toward my grandparents' room,

Uncle Richie motioned for me to join him in the kitchen. Every counter was covered with food—mostly cakes and pies and cookies. It looked like a Betty Crocker Cook-Off.

"Help yourself," my uncle told me as he poured himself another cup of coffee.

But I couldn't eat. I knew my grandfather was in his room dying. On a visit just two weeks before, my grandfather's condition had shocked me. A year earlier he had retired from the business, turning it over to my uncle. Then he and Grandma had bought a motor home and started traveling the country—a long cherished dream. But before they could see all they wanted to see, my grandfather was diagnosed with cancer. He went to the Mayo Clinic for treatment, but the doctors sent him home without hope for a cure. Now the family was gathering to say their good-byes.

After a while I went into my grandfather's room. As was typical in our house of silence and secrets, no one had prepared me for what cancer had done to Grandpa. That big, robust man had been reduced to skin and bones, too frail to raise his arms and hug me. Stunned, I thought, *he really is dying*. I held his hand and cried. The one adult with whom I felt safe was now leaving me forever. There would be no more summers picking apples with my grandfather, no more stories at his knee, no more warm hugs and smiles.

Later, as I sat at the kitchen table, the silence was deafening. No one was talking. No radio, no television, nothing to disturb the quiet of impending death. Even Aunt Sandra was quiet, sitting at the table and picking at a piece of chocolate cake.

Aunt Sandra was mentally handicapped and, though she was a grown woman, had the mind of a four-year-old. Normally she was exuberant and happy and smiling at everything and everyone. But not tonight. Somehow she knew this was not the time for smiles. It was a time for tears.

For years Grandpa's home had been the only refuge I had known, especially after we moved from the house on the Wolf River to our new home on Robin Avenue. Now I had my own room and no longer was buffered by my brother's room. Within days of moving into the new house, Daddy began coming into my room at night. Most of the time I would pretend I was sleeping until he finished and left.

I felt a heavy hand on my shoulder and jumped.

"You okay, kid?" Uncle Richie asked.

I could only nod while dislodging the knot in my throat.

He pulled out a chair and sat down, running his hands through his hair as he blew out a heavy sigh full of grief. "Yeah, this is tough on all of us. I know you were close to him."

Tears streamed down my face.

He slowly turned his coffee mug, as if searching for something else to say. "I heard you have a new brother."

"Matthew," I replied softly. He was just a few weeks old and the cutest thing I'd ever seen. When Nadine was little, I enjoyed holding her and feeding her, but Matthew was just so sweet and fragile. Maybe Nadine had been that sweet too, but I just couldn't remember.

Then my mom returned, buttoning her coat. "Let's go, Tina."

She embraced my grandmother briefly and then stood and waited while I slipped into my coat.

I gave Uncle Richie a quick hug and followed my mom out of the kitchen.

I had seen my mom cry from time to time—when Daddy hit her, sometimes when he yelled at her, or when she was in pain—but this was different. Silent tears tracked down her face, her eyes were downcast, her movements jerky and disoriented. I had to help her find her keys in her coat pocket.

My mom had always been close to her dad. She loved him dearly, just as I did, so this was going to be extremely difficult for her. I wanted to comfort her, to tell her everything was going to be okay, but in my experiences to that point—nothing ever got to be "okay."

When we got back home to Shawano, Mom retired to her room. Daddy was in there with her for a little while, then he came out, turned on a football game, and told us to go play quietly somewhere. We were more than happy to comply.

A few days later, we got the call that Grandpa had died. Mom was so despondent she could barely stand. She wore a pair of oddly enormous black sunglasses and couldn't stop crying.

Watching my grandfather's casket being lowered into the ground was enough to break my heart. I knew the sad moment would be forever etched in my mind—the flowers, the shiny wood, my grandmother sobbing in my uncle's arms, Mom hiding her grief behind those big glasses, the coffin slowly disappearing into that hole in the ground.

After the funeral everyone went back to my grandparents'

house to eat. The house was filled with friends, family, and neighbors. They stood around in tiny clutches of two and three and talked about how fast my grandfather declined, how tragic it was that he barely had a year to travel after retiring, how much my grandmother would miss him, how sad it all was for everyone.

I was one heartbroken little girl.

Spring 1981
Shawano, Wisconsin

It was one of those beautiful spring weekends when people find any excuse to be out and about, taking advantage of brilliant blue skies and a warm sun. All the windows were open and you could hear the warm, happy sounds of Wisconsin shaking off another long winter—kids laughing, dogs barking, and lawnmower engines up and down the street.

Kyle, Whitney, and Nadine were outside somewhere, playing in the backyard maybe or somewhere down the street with neighborhood friends. I wanted to be out but was stuck inside with a list of chores long enough to keep me inside until dinner.

I was in the kitchen folding towels at the table while my mom was sweeping the floor. She set the broom aside and closed her eyes, massaging her temples with her fingertips. Pale and drawn, I could see the pain of a headache etched in her face.

"You okay?" I asked.

She shook her head gently as if it hurt to move it and stepped into the living room. "I'm going to go lie down for a little while," I heard her tell my dad. "Can you keep an eye on the kids?"

"Yeah," he replied.

A soft breeze moved into the room, fluttering the kitchen curtains and caressing my cheek. I stared with longing at the yard beyond the back door. I was the oldest of five kids now, and as the oldest, I was expected to pick up the slack, do more chores, and handle more responsibility. Sometimes it wasn't so bad, but on a day like today, I wanted to be with my friends, talking about the latest music and teachers and boys and clothes and makeup and all the things I could understand now that I was thirteen and officially a teenager.

"Tina!" my dad called out.

With a sigh, I tossed a towel down on the table and walked over to the archway leading to the living room. "Yes?"

"Come here."

I could see it in his eyes, but I couldn't believe it. Mom was just down the hall in her room. Surely he couldn't be thinking about this with her right in the next room. I had to be wrong.

Reluctantly I moved closer and he reached out and grabbed me, pulling me down on the sofa. I couldn't believe he was doing this while my mom was home. She could walk in at any time. Was he crazy?

But he seemed not to be the least bit bothered, his focus on one thing only. I closed my eyes and tried to take my mind far away from where I was and what was happening, but thoughts kept intruding—Mom was in the next room. Why is he doing this with Mom in the house? She could walk out here at any moment and then what?

I heard a sharp gasp. I opened my eyes and stared straight into my mother's horrified expression.

I'm pretty sure I stopped breathing, but I was in such shock, I honestly can't remember how I reacted.

However, there was a look on Mom's face that I will never forget as long as I live. Her lips were moving, saying my dad's name over and over in horror. Then she turned and fled from the room.

Daddy jumped up and ran after her, leaving me there on the sofa. I sat up, straightening my clothes with trembling fingers. What would happen now? How bad was this fight going to be?

For the better part of an hour I sat on the sofa, my hands clenching and unclenching, emotions jumping from fear to terror to shame to horror to fear again. It was as though I were hanging from some cliff, ready to drop into a bottomless pit. What was happening back in their bedroom? I wasn't sure I even wanted to know.

My dad came out first, barely glancing in my direction as he headed for the front door, carrying a suitcase. "Finish the laundry, Tina." He walked out, slamming the door behind him.

Slowly I stood up and walked into the kitchen, scrambling to understand. *What now?*

A few minutes later I picked up the stack of towels and headed down the hall to put them away. I passed Mom coming out of her room. I studied her face, waiting for her to say something, but she turned her head away from me and didn't speak.

I was devastated. This was all my fault and Mom was never going to forgive me.

"Mom?"

She continued down the hall as if I had never spoken. I knew she'd heard me, but you wouldn't have known it from the way she walked on, disappearing into the kitchen.

I shoved the towels into the linen closet and hurried back to the kitchen. Mom was taking potatoes out of a bag and setting them on the counter.

"Mommy?"

Pulling the utensil drawer open, she pulled out the potato peeler and turned her back to me.

I was crushed. I had ruined everything. Now Mom hated me. She'd never speak to me again.

I had become invisible and my heart went cold. I was turned away, guilty of unspeakable crimes against my mom. How could I explain that it was never what I wanted, that I had no choice? That if I had told, no one would speak to me or listen to me or want me around? How could I explain the ache in my soul when in my mother's eyes I no longer existed?

For days the silence echoed like a judge's gavel. Guilty. Guilty. Guilty. Then one evening my mother came into my bedroom. "We're going to talk to someone from the church."

"Pastor Tim?"

She shook her head, scowling. "No way am I letting Pastor Tim know about this. Not him and not the church. We'll go to a church down in Appleton and talk to someone there. No one can ever know about this. Do you understand me?"

I didn't know what to say. There were emotions running through my young brain that I couldn't understand. I had no experience, no insight, nothing to draw on to deal with this unfolding drama. My mom had finally caught my dad molesting me and made him leave the house. So why were we going to talk to someone at the church about it? What would I have to tell? And why?

Finally, I managed to sort through all the raging emotions and ask a simple question. "When are we going?"

She stared at me for a moment as if there was something she wanted to say, but she couldn't find the words. Then she turned away. "We have an appointment for Wednesday."

A few days later we drove to Appleton, which was about an hour's drive away. I sat in the backseat, invisible to my mom.

The pastor of the Lutheran church greeted me with a reserved smile and invited us into his office. There were two chairs in front of his desk, a small sofa in the corner, and more books than I'd seen anywhere outside the library. Suddenly, to my surprise, my dad walked into the room and sat down in the chair next to my mother. That left me with the small sofa, so I went over and sat down. I felt as if I'd been shoved over in a corner, once again not worthy of being seen or heard.

After a few initial comments, the pastor asked the reason for the meeting, and my mom started off explaining how she had walked in on us in the living room. The pastor then turned to my dad and asked him how long this had been going on.

"Just a little while," my dad said softly. "I never meant for this to happen."

My mother's mouth pressed flat and her lips all but disappeared as she glared at my dad.

I could feel my face burning with shame as my dad talked about his lack of control and how sorry he was and about some of the more intimate details of the abuse.

The pastor listened carefully, but I couldn't read his face. He showed no emotion at all, but every once in a while I would see him wince. I didn't know if it was out of sympathy for me or just shock at some of the things he was hearing. I imagine a pastor doesn't often hear such sexually explicit detail.

With hands folded in front of him on the desk, the pastor took a deep breath. "Why did you touch her?"

My dad glanced briefly over at me and then shrugged. "I don't know for sure. I couldn't help it. There was just something about her."

Once again, I felt helpless, naked, as though my parents and this stranger were dissecting my soul. I started crying. I couldn't help it. I felt so dirty, so filthy, so incredibly ashamed.

My mother looked over at me, and I believed she was embarrassed at my sobbing. In spite of not wanting to disappoint her, I couldn't stop the tears. I wanted to be indifferent, cocooned, aloof. I wanted to bury the feelings and pretend I was just fine with it all, but my emotions were stronger than my resolve, tougher than my intentions.

"Let her cry it out," the pastor said, handing me a box of tissues. "She needs to."

My mother compressed her lips, gave me a disapproving glance, and turned back to the pastor. "What now?"

"I should report this to the authorities, but I don't see any need for that." He looked over at my dad. "You've come in voluntarily and confessed. It won't be happening again, is that correct?"

"Absolutely."

He turned back to my mother. "The church expects that as a good Christian woman, you forgive your husband for his sins and take him back. The family needs to be held together if it's at all possible."

My mother didn't look at all pleased with the outcome. "I'm not ready to have him back yet. I need to know that this is never going to happen again."

The pastor nodded. "I can appreciate that. Why don't we meet once a week for a while and see how it goes?"

He turned to my dad. "What about you? Can you stop this compulsive behavior?"

"I've tried a couple of times and failed, but yes . . . I think that now, with God's help, I can stop."

The pastor pulled out a calendar and studied it. "I think we should all meet every Wednesday afternoon for a while. We'll work on putting this all behind us."

A few months later, my dad moved out of the hotel he'd been staying in and back into the house. We continued driving down to Appleton for counseling. Sure enough, my dad left me alone.

Little by little, things began to get back to normal, or what passed for normal around our house. Mom started talking to me again, although it wasn't quite the same as it had been before. There was always an unspoken tension between us—me wanting to explain how I felt and her not wanting to discuss it at all.

Then she dropped the bomb one evening while I was watching TV. "We're sending you to Fox Valley Lutheran School in Appleton."

I was stunned. Appleton was over an hour's drive away. "Why?" I asked, my eyes filling with tears.

"Your dad and I have made the decision. You don't get to ask questions. I called today and enrolled you."

"But how will I get there?"

"Your dad will drive you down in the morning and pick you up on his way home from work. You will sit in the library or the principal's office doing your homework until he arrives to take you home."

She turned and left the room.

For just over a year, my dad would drive me down to Appleton and drop me off at school on his way to work. I wanted to get involved in school activities, but with it taking more than two hours a day just for the commute, that was out of the question. So I sat in the school and did my homework as the clock ticked slowly away, waiting for Dad to pick me up each evening. I was barely ever at home anymore, except for weekends. Dad and I left early and didn't get home until late. I'd have dinner and then it was time to get ready for bed.

I felt completely cut off from my family, but I was about to be pushed even farther away.

My English teacher had a talk with my dad, letting him know that I was often late to her class because he dropped me off too late in the morning. Rather than his making the effort to get on the road earlier, it was decided that I would move to Appleton and board with a local family during the week, coming home only on the weekends. I was miserable and lonely.

Then I met Derek. He was one of the cutest boys in the school, or at least I thought so. I practically danced on air when he gave me an I.D. bracelet with his name on it, which meant we were officially going steady.

Like most young romances, our relationship had its extreme highs and lows. During the week, it was all about the high of being with him, slipping notes to each other in the hall, gazing at each other across the cafeteria table. On the weekends, it was the low of being separated from him, going home to be with my family. The biggest low came when I returned to school one Monday morning to face the gossip.

I was at my locker, putting my coat and lunch away, when two girls I sometimes hung with came up to me, all bouncy smiles and giggles.

"You should have been at the party, Tina. It was great!"

"Yeah, maybe if you'd been there, Derek wouldn't have been making out with your best friend."

My heart hit the floor with a thud so loud I was surprised no one heard it but me. "Derek? He was cheating on me?"

One of the girls had the decency to look embarrassed as she nodded. "He was dancing with her and they were making out and everything. I saw them kissing."

Well, needless to say, I gave Derek his bracelet back. He apologized and agreed it was a stupid thing to do. Even though we made up, it was never the same after that.

I didn't return to Fox Valley the next year. My parents told me that the tuition money would be better spent for college, so I moved home and transferred to the local high school in Shawano.

That year I was able to go out on real dates with boys, but any boy that wanted to take me out had to go through my dad first. Ironically, he turned into Mr. Protective when it came to my dates. He would grill them for twenty minutes or so on their plans for the future, their parents, their interests and hobbies, before finally allowing the date to proceed. The funny thing was, the boys he liked and gave permission to date me were usually the ones who were lying through their teeth and would take me to drinking parties rather than the movies they'd said we were going to.

By this time I had grown into a submissive, fearful young woman always seeking to please. My deepest fear was to be rejected or abandoned. My parents decided everything for me, from whom I could date to the school classes I would take. My mom made it clear. "I'm going to make sure you go to college and have options in your life. You won't be trapped like I was."

It didn't matter that I longed to take an art class; my parents decided I was to take physiology instead. I lived on automatic pilot, with my parents at the controls of my life.

Right before my junior year, I applied for a job at McDonald's. The day before the interview my mother bought me a black London Fog spring coat. She prepped me on what to say during the interview and picked out what I should wear. She made it clear that she wanted me to get this job and that if I got it, she'd be proud of me.

I got the message loud and clear. Not only did I get the job, but from then on my work ethic was top-notch. I would outwork any other employee, push myself to the limit, work long hours if I had to, anything to make sure I would shine as an employee. Then maybe my mother would be proud of me enough to love me again.

After my dad stopped bothering me for sexual favors and my mom began acting more friendly toward me, my life felt almost like that of a normal teenager.

"Mom, come on," I said excitedly. In fact I was so pumped about taking my driver's test and getting my license that morning that I could barely get my sweater buttoned. Finally, I'd be able to drive! Freedom! Independence! Fun! How cool was that? I planned to get a better job, then buy a car—and soon everything would be perfect.

I stuck my head in my mother's room. She was sitting on the bed, staring at a box in her lap, a strange expression on her face.

"Mom?"

"Come in and shut the door, Tina. We need to talk."

Fear immediately overtook my youthful anticipation and squeezed out the tentative joy that had started to build. I pushed the door closed but didn't move any closer to my mom.

She patted the bed. "Come. Sit."

I slowly walked over, my feet forcing me forward. "What's going on, Mom?"

"I just need to talk to you about something before we leave, that's all."

"About what?"

She sighed and lifted some papers out of the box.

"Is that my birth certificate?" I reached out for it but at first, she resisted letting go of it. Then she released it.

"I need to explain."

But I was already reading it. I was born on April 9, 1968, in Menominee, Michigan. My mother's maiden name was listed on the form. And my father—"Mom. This is wrong."

She shook her head, wringing her hands in her lap. "No, it's not."

I looked over at her, totally confused. "But this says that my father is David Prezewrocki. I don't understand."

"I was married before, Tina. You were too young to remember your real father. We divorced eight months after Kyle was born."

There it was. Another secret coming out to suck the air from the room, stealing my breath, scattering my thoughts. I had been raised by a stepfather.

So *he* wasn't my father at all. He was my stepfather. Nadine and Matthew were my half-sister and -brother. Kyle, Whitney, and I had a different father. It wasn't my real dad who had sexually molested me. It had been the man whom my mother had married after divorcing my father.

"So my name is really Tina Marie Prezewrocki?"

"Yes."

"Then why have I been using *his* name all this time? Why did you let me think he was my father?"

"You were so young at the time. We thought it best that you have no memories of your real father, that you just forget him."

"Forget him?" I wanted to scream. "The Christmas tree. Who burned it down?"

Her eyes widened. I guess she didn't realize that I did have memories of my real father, memories that I had nearly convinced myself were fantasies, dreams, and lies. "Your father. You remember that?"

"I remember. He's the one that shot my dog too, isn't he?"

She nodded. "I can't believe you remember."

"Where is he? Why hasn't he tried to see us?"

There was that expression again, and my heart jumped in my chest. "He's dead, Tina."

"How? I want to know. I want to know everything."

She gave me the whole story, holding nothing back.

My mother and David met in her junior year of high school. She had been attracted to his intelligence and fell deeply in love. When she found out she was pregnant, she hid it for almost five months, but eventually the truth came out and her mother had told her, "You made your bed; now you have to lie in it."

David and my mom married on November 23, 1967, and she dropped out of school. After I was born, Mom went back to finish high school. She and David went on to have two more children in quick succession. Whitney was born in September of 1969 and Kyle in September of 1970.

As a twenty-one-year-old father of three, David turned to alcohol to help him cope with the pressure. It wasn't long before things turned nasty. He hurt Mom and his rages were violent, violent enough that even at such a young age, I had fleeting memories of him forcing my mother to make me watch him shoot my dog.

In 1971 they divorced, and three months later she married again. Meanwhile, David continued to have problems. He was in and out of the Newberry Psychiatric Hospital in Luce County, Michigan. He said he missed his children and wanted to see them, but my stepfather had moved us away from Michigan and down to Ashwaubenon, Wisconsin. The day after my fifth birthday, my real father took a gun and shot himself in the chest. He did try to call for help, but his phone was on a party line and someone else was talking on it. By the time the ambulance arrived, it was too late. He died forty-five minutes after reaching the hospital.

"Tina, listen to me."

My hands were shaking so badly, I could barely hold my birth certificate. My real father, the man who had given me life, had been so depressed at losing me that he'd killed himself. My real dad had loved me. He'd wanted to see me. My stepfather had hurt me. He took my childish, innocent trust and twisted it into some sick, perverted thing.

I realize now that I was idealizing my real father, but after the years of sexual abuse, anything looked better than what I had.

"Tina!"

I realized then that I was crying. I reached for a tissue from the box on my mother's nightstand and wiped my tears away. How different life might have been if I'd been able to see my real dad after the divorce! His drunken rages might not have been very different from my stepfather's violent rages, but maybe I wouldn't have been sexually molested.

My mother took my hand and squeezed it. "Listen to me, Tina. No one can know. Do you hear me? Kyle and Whitney can't know about this. I'll tell them later when they're older, but you have to keep this a secret."

I could only stare at her. How many secrets was this family going to harbor? No one could know about the violence. No one could know about the abuse. No one could know my stepfather was a child molester. No one could know he wasn't my real father.

Secrets on top of secrets on top of lies on top of lies—all to be hidden away behind a happy family facade.

chapter three

Bad Choices

I started dating Terry the summer before college. We met at one of the local teen parties. My mother didn't care for Terry but when she voiced her objection, I replied, "I'm just dating the guy, Mom, not marrying him."

In September I left for the University of Wisconsin–Green Bay. My mom helped me move into my dorm room. When I had filled out the school housing questionnaire, I asked to be paired with a conservative roommate, because I didn't want someone who was going to be more interested in dating and parties than her studies. My roommate turned out to be a farm girl from Pulaski, who was even more conservative than I was. She was intelligent, quiet, and kept to herself.

My tennis coach was a wonderful woman who opened up a whole new world for me. She also coached cross-country skiing and taught health courses. I loved being on the tennis team. We traveled August through October, thus limiting my study time, but I still managed to keep my grades up. Most of my grades were As, but if participating in tennis forced me to get an occasional B or C, the sacrifice was worth it to me.

Then October gave way to November, tennis was over, and the traveling stopped. Like most college students, I was broke, so I went home on the weekends with my dirty laundry and ate as much of those wonderful home-cooked meals as I could to make up for barely eating during the week. Unfortunately, tension developed between my youngest sister, Nadine, and me, and she made sure I knew that as far as she was concerned, I wasn't welcome at home. I started seeing my family less and less and missing them more and more.

After I left for college, my relationship with Terry grew strained as well. He wanted to go to college too, but his father expected him to take over the family business. My taking the road that he so wanted to take resulted in an uneasy jealousy. Even so, we tried to work around it. He took me to nice restaurants, sent me roses, and wrote me little love notes. Despite the miles between us, I believed our love could overcome whatever roadblocks we would face.

By early December I was feeling more alone than I'd felt since being sent off to live in Appleton. I didn't have a car, so I was stuck at school most of the time. My only relief from the loneliness and boredom was to get on the bus and ride down to the mall. One afternoon, while Christmas shopping, I wandered over to a rack of blouses and saw one that I really liked. Folding it up, I shoved it down in one of my shopping bags. As I made my way toward the exit, I heard footsteps rushing up behind me, but I kept going.

As my hand hit the door, two undercover security guards grabbed me and hauled me roughly up to the second-floor security office. While they waited for the police to arrive, they put me in a small room with just a desk and a couple of chairs.

Terrified, I sat there crying. A few minutes later, a police officer on one side of me and the two store security officers on the other side grilled me mercilessly.

"What else did you steal?"

"Did you steal all the rest of the stuff in this bag?"

"Have you been shoplifting for a long time?"

"Didn't think you'd get caught, did you?"

Bombarded with questions, it was all I could do to insist that this was the first time and the only thing I'd ever taken. Mortified at being caught, I was sobbing as I turned to the police officer. "My dad . . . if he finds out I've done this . . ." I sobbed harder, more upset at the thought of disappointing and embarrassing my family at that point than the actual charges. "You can't let him find out. Please."

Saying nothing, the police officer wrote out the citation, charging me with shoplifting. I was required to pay a fine and appear before the judge.

A couple of weeks later, I went home for Christmas, and my

stepfather cornered me in the family room while the rest of the family was busy elsewhere.

"Tina, we need to talk."

"Sure." I turned off the television as he settled in his chair.

"I found out about the shoplifting."

My breath caught in my chest. "How did you find out?"

"The officer called me. As the father of two teenage girls, he was concerned about you. He says that he felt something more was going on here than you just wanting a blouse you couldn't afford, that maybe something is bothering you."

I shook my head. "I'm fine."

"Why did you do it then?"

"I don't know."

He studied me for a moment and then sighed in one of those ways that was as familiar as my mother's pot roast. "Well, I talked to the officer, and we decided to take this off your record. He knew you weren't there purposely to steal, so he's going to give you a break. But don't ever do something like that again."

"I won't. I promise."

"This is just not like you, Tina."

I swallowed hard as the tears welled up. I had disappointed my family, and now my stepfather was going to cover up my mistake to protect me. I was an adult. I was supposed to be handling my own problems. Maybe if I'd realized at that moment that the shoplifting was a precursor to a series of behaviors that would appear whenever I needed to cry out for help, whenever I was feeling abandoned, rejected, or desperately alone, it would have given me insight. But I didn't know that a pattern was developing.

A few months later my mom called to inform me I had another problem to deal with.

"I thought you should know that Terry is dating Marlie. You remember Marlie, don't you? She was your best friend in high school, wasn't she?"

"How do you know that?" I asked her, unable or unwilling to believe the news. I preferred to think Mom might simply be hoping to break us up.

"Nadine saw them together. Your sister wouldn't lie about this, Tina. Check it out for yourself."

And so I did. I called Marlie's house, and my heart sank when she said Terry was there. I asked her to put Terry on the phone. He didn't deny anything, but I think he felt bad that he'd been caught. It was a double betrayal. Not only had my boyfriend cheated on me, but it was with someone I considered a close friend.

A few months later Terry showed up at my dorm on a Saturday night. "I need to talk to you," he said.

I looked at the clock. It was after eleven. "Terry, it's late."

"I know, but I really need to talk to someone. Please."

So, we sat down on the stairs. "Marlie's pregnant," he told me. "I didn't mean for it to happen. I thought we had it worked out, that she'd agree to get an abortion, but she said she talked to your mom and now she's decided to keep it."

That didn't surprise me. Marlie had a better relationship with my mother than she did with her own, and it wasn't the first time my friend had gone to my mom for advice.

"Are you going to marry her?" I asked.

He shook his head. "No, I broke up with her. If she wants to have it, that's her decision, but I don't love her like that." Suddenly he broke into tears. "Everything is just so messed up, Tina. My grandfather just died and you know how close he and I were. And now this confusion with Marlie. I just don't know how to handle any of this."

I put my arms around him and tried to comfort him. He looked up, his eyes so dark with emotion it tugged on my heart.

"You know I never stopped loving you, Tina. That's the problem. I was so jealous of you going off to college while I had to stay home and work. You're off traveling with the tennis team and doing so great, and my life is stuck in this awful rut. I guess I turned to Marlie as a way of lashing out. I should never have done it. I didn't mean to hurt you and I did. Worse . . . I lost you."

With that heartfelt speech, my feelings for Terry stirred. I took him back.

During summer break, I took a job cleaning apartments. One day while cleaning, I felt faint and nearly blacked out. I was physically fit, and it was unlike me to feel frail or weak. I began to suspect I might be pregnant, but even that seemed unlikely since I was on the pill. I took a test at a Planned Parenthood Clinic, which confirmed my fears. I expected them to give me some counseling, some options, some advice. Instead, I was simply told where to go in Appleton to have an abortion. Nothing was mentioned about keeping the baby or possibly giving it up for adoption. Abortion was the only avenue offered.

I wasn't sure what to do. My parents had high career expectations for me after I graduated from college, and I'd be letting them down. My mother had gotten pregnant in high school, and I knew that my pregnancy while in college would disappoint her.

The only one I could talk to was Terry. In spite of the matter-of-fact clinical advice I'd received at Planned Parenthood, the idea of taking away the life growing inside me felt so wrong. But the more Terry and I talked about it, the more I realized that having a baby at this point in our lives would be a huge mistake. We promised ourselves that someday we'd do it right. We'd get married and then start a family.

So I made the appointment at the clinic in Appleton. It was a tiny clinic in the middle of nowhere with five or six people picketing outside the place. The doctor didn't speak much English. The nurse didn't seem to care about anything at all, as if she walked in a protective bubble to keep herself from feeling. They put my feet in the stirrups, gave me a painkiller, and told me to hold on to two straps. Then I heard something that sounded like a big vacuum. I was absolutely terrified, but neither the doctor nor the nurse offered so much as one word of comfort or reassurance.

Afterward Terry drove me to his parents' house, where I was able to sleep for a couple of hours. I ended up staying with his grandmother the rest of the summer, cleaning and painting for her, unable to go home and face my parents.

My parents never counseled me to wait to have sex until marriage, probably because they both knew I wasn't a virgin anyway. The only sex education I ever had came when I was sixteen or seventeen. My mother told me that if I was going to have sex, I needed to use birth control.

Toward the end of the summer, I finally went home to see my family. When I was getting ready to leave, Terry went out to the car while I said good-bye to everyone. My mother was in the kitchen, doing dishes. I gave her a hug.

"I can't believe you're staying with that boy," she said, her face tight with anger. She reached for a dish towel, wiping her hands as she glared at me. "Let me tell you something, young lady. If you walk out that door and leave with him, you will no longer be welcome in this house and you will no longer be a part of this family. Do I make myself clear? I will not allow you to just ruin your life over someone like him."

It's not that I wanted Terry more than I wanted my family—not at all—but I was angry that she was trying to take control of my life and that she would give me such a hurtful ultimatum.

I walked out the door, got in the car with Terry, and left.

If only she had sat me down and talked to me with a bit of kindness and concern about what she was feeling. If only she'd explained that she felt strongly that Terry would only hurt me again and again. If only she'd told me she felt I'd been hurt enough in this life. But to tell me that I would never be allowed back in my family if my choice displeased her was just more than I could stand.

Terry and I got an apartment less than two miles from my parents' home. It was hard being so close and not being able to see them or my brothers and sisters. I knew I was making the wrong choice to stay with Terry, but it was a decision I made out of anger and spite, not love. And when he asked me to get engaged, I quickly said yes.

I was in the second semester of my sophomore year in college. Without a car and living in Shawano instead of Green Bay, I had to drive Terry's car back and forth to school. I chose my classes so that they would all be on Tuesdays and Thursdays and I would need Terry's car only two days a week. On those days I would drop Terry off at work, drive over to Green Bay for a full day of classes, and then rush back to pick him up.

Once again, I felt isolated and alone. Terry didn't want me to befriend anyone from college or stay after school to talk to anyone.

On Monday, Wednesday, and Friday, I sat at the kitchen table, doing homework. There was no one to talk to and I was starting to feel trapped. Once again, someone else was controlling my life. This time it was Terry. However, without any distractions, I made straight *A*s that semester.

Terry and I were spending less and less time together. On the days he was off, he would leave early in the morning to work out at the gym. Then he started going out with his friends, not coming home until after two in the morning. He assured me that he was just hanging out with buddies, but deep inside I think I knew the truth.

One day I was out running—something I'd always loved doing—and began to cry out to God. "Please get me out of this situation, God. I hate it. I'm so miserable and I don't know what to do."

It was the first time in my life I understood what a true depression felt like. I missed my family. I missed my friends. I hated not having my family's support. I hated being rejected by my mother once again.

Then I found out I was pregnant again. This time I wasn't as surprised. I had been unable to afford birth control, but we'd tried to be careful. Obviously it hadn't worked.

I could hear my mother talking to me about birth control back in high school. "Be careful, Tina. I don't want you to get pregnant and ruin your life like I did." I was the child she had gotten pregnant with, so it always made me feel as if I had ruined her life.

I knew Terry was cheating on me, and I knew I wanted to get out of this relationship. So when it came time to tell Terry, I used the same excuse we'd used before. "It's not the right time. After we get married, then we'll start our family." But this time it was so traumatic that I have blocked out all memory of what happened after Terry and I walked into the clinic.

After the second abortion, during the summer break from classes, I started working at the Shawano Paper Mill. That's where I met Scott.

Scott was a great looking man in his late twenties, over

six feet tall with dark brown hair and blue eyes. He walked into my life at one of its lowest points and offered me a way out. He helped me move out of the apartment I shared with Terry and offered to let me stay at his place until I could get out on my own. It wasn't my first choice—it was my only choice. I couldn't go back home and I couldn't stay with Terry any longer. I'd had enough. I went back to Terry's one morning a little after seven to get the last of my things and found him sleeping with another woman. Worse, it was someone I knew.

I don't know if she knew I was engaged to Terry or not, but I just threw this into the large, mental pile of betrayals I'd experienced in my life. Though my mom was wrong about many things, she was right about Terry.

My relationship with Scott turned out to be an easy and comfortable one. We would just sit and talk for hours, and I so enjoyed that about him. Here was someone who was actually interested in what I had to say, who valued my opinion. He started going to church with me. He seemed proud to have me on his arm and even took me to meet his family.

Now I just had to make things right with my mom. My mother had a tendency to use the "tough love" approach to child rearing, and while it worked fine with my younger siblings, it didn't work at all with me. And even though I knew that her ultimatums were probably more of her tough love, I was always afraid that one day she might actually mean them and there would be no going back for me.

My hands were sweating as I picked up the phone and dialed. It rang once. Twice. And then I heard my mother's voice. "Hello?"

"Mom?"

"Why are you calling here? I told you . . ."

"I broke up with Terry." I cut her off, my words tumbling out fast in the hope she would hear me out before she hung up. "I left him."

There was a long silence, and I almost thought she had hung up. "Mom?"

"When did this happen?"

"A couple weeks ago."

"And you're just now calling me to tell me?"

I took a deep breath, almost smiling. She wasn't rejecting me. "I wasn't sure if you'd take my call."

"I just didn't want him hurting you. Do you understand?"

"I do now."

The summer passed and I went back for my junior year of college and back to the tennis team. After moving everything into my room at school, I broke up with Scott. I felt bad about hurting him, but he was starting to talk marriage and I wasn't ready.

Midway through my junior year, I could look back at those two years with Terry and see things more clearly. I hadn't realized how severely I'd been suffering from depression until I was free from him and feeling rare but wonderful flutters of happiness again. I was in control of my life, and I swore I'd never let anyone control me like that again. I wasn't going to lay my heart on the line and be dependent on someone else.

Though I'd tried to tell myself that I'd just "had a couple of necessary medical procedures," the abortions left two open wounds in my soul, and they were still bleeding, still hurting, and still haunting me. I discovered that when life starts and ends within a woman's body, there's no easy way around the grief. No amount of rationalization could erase the reality that I'd ended the lives of two babies.

I wanted love, but was no longer sure I knew what love was. What did real love look like? As much as I wanted love, I knew I didn't trust it. Or maybe I just didn't trust myself to recognize the real thing when it came along. So I built up walls around my heart, unwilling to let anyone get close to me again.

chapter 4

Trusting Love

January 1989
Green Bay, Wisconsin

My friend Jody and I wove our way through the crowd to the bar at Sneakers, a local hangout for the college crowd. After we ordered our drinks, we leaned against the polished wood and looked around the room, checking out who was there and whom we might know.

"See that cute guy over there?" I nudged Jody. "Didn't we see him over at Top Shelf last weekend?"

The week before, a few members of the tennis team had gathered at the Top Shelf after practice, and some of the members of the golf team had been in there as well. There was one guy on the team who really stood out.

And here he was, catching my eye again.

Jody looked him over carefully. "Yep, I think that's the same guy. He's kinda cute, isn't he?"

"Sure is."

She gave me one of those calculating looks and then, putting both her hands on my back, pushed me up to him. Jody was a lot more outgoing than I was and thought nothing of introducing herself to anyone, anywhere. I envied her carefree attitude.

"Hi," she said to him with a big smile. "I'm Jody and this is my friend Tina. She really wanted to meet you."

What I really wanted to do right then was sink through the floor and disappear, but he flashed a big smile that charmed me right out of my embarrassment. "I've wanted to meet her too." He held out his hand to me. "I'm Daniel Zahn."

"You're on the golf team, aren't you?"

"I am. And you're on the tennis team. So where did you go to high school?"

Jody gave me a little pat on the shoulder and wandered off. I barely noticed. "Fox Valley Lutheran and then Shawano."

Daniel's eyes seemed to light up. "Really? Me too."

We found a table and sat down to talk. We discovered we had a lot in common and quite a few mutual acquaintances, which kept the conversation moving. Then suddenly he grabbed my arm. "Dance with me."

He held me way too close and I didn't like that, but I chalked it up to maybe a beer or two too many. I was willing to overlook this, since he was such a nice guy. Time flew and soon it was closing time. Jody, Dina, Daniel, and I walked out to the parking lot. Jody suggested we all go over to the Country Kitchen for breakfast. Daniel volunteered to drive me over. Jody and Dina would go in Jody's car and meet us there.

However, when Daniel and I arrived at the restaurant, Jody wasn't there. While we were waiting for her, Daniel grew very quiet.

"Is everything okay? I mean, if you have to leave or something, I understand."

"No, no," he assured me. "I was just thinking of my grandfather. We were pretty tight and he passed away recently. Heart attack. It was pretty unexpected."

"I'm so sorry."

"Thanks. I miss him a lot. He's the one that taught me to play golf."

"Really? You like golf a lot, don't you?"

"More than a lot, I suppose. I think I'd rather be playing golf than just about anything else."

"I know what you mean. I'm that way about running."

We finally realized that Jody had set us up and that she wasn't coming. We were enjoying each other so much that we went ahead and ordered breakfast. Then Daniel drove me to my dorm. I was willing to be let out in the parking lot, but he insisted on walking me to my door. "Listen, Tina, I'd really like to see you again. Can I have your number?"

"Sure. I'd like that, Daniel."

Daniel and I took it slowly, which was good for me because I wasn't ready to jump into anything that smacked of serious romance. We'd pass in the halls at school and he'd say hi. Sometimes he'd pull me aside to chat for a few minutes before rushing off to his next class. Most of our friends didn't even think of us as a couple since we were only seeing each other occasionally. He'd ask me out to dinner or a movie, or we'd run into each other at a party and end up spending the evening together.

Almost two years passed and we were seeing a lot of each other, but I still kept a close watch on my heart. Love couldn't be trusted; ultimately it would only lead to hurt. So when Daniel planned a trip down to Lacrosse and invited me to go with him, I declined, afraid of what might happen. I just didn't want to be put in an uncomfortable position.

I had been back from spring break a couple of days when I got a call from Daniel. He was at a party and had been drinking a bit too much and wanted to know if I'd pick him up and drive him home. I agreed.

We ended up back at my apartment, talking most of the night away. It was the first time Daniel had ever opened up and really talked about his feelings.

"I really love you, Teen. I want to marry you."

"Dan, you barely know me."

I expected some kind of denial, but instead his eyes filled with tears. "I know you, Teen. I've been in love with you for a long time. Just waiting for you to be ready to love me."

Once again, I tried to brush aside his declaration, but I could feel my defenses starting to melt. "You've had too much to drink. Once you sober up you'll . . ."

"No! I'm just tipsy enough to throw caution aside and admit what I've been feeling for you all along. I know you've been hurt and I know you have trouble trusting, so I've been going slowly. But I love you, Teen. I love you with all my heart and I want to marry you."

I wanted to believe him. I really did. But it was so hard. He had given me time and space to heal. He hadn't pressured me with demands or jealousy. He was intelligent and sweet and considerate. I'd never known him to so much as look at another woman, which went a long way toward helping me trust him, but could I really trust these feelings? Could I dare to have hope, to put my heart on the line?

We started spending more time together and eventually met each other's parents. My parents liked Daniel right away, and our parents liked each other.

After a while Daniel popped the question, I said yes, and he put a ring on my finger. Both sets of parents were thrilled, but I was still questioning myself, my feelings, and my decision. Was I just marrying this guy because my parents approved of him, because he was trustworthy and stable, and because I knew he wouldn't cheat on me? How could I marry him if I wasn't sure I was really in love with him?

I pushed aside my doubts and we set the date for June 26.

After he graduated, Daniel started working at a car dealership. He seemed to live in an obvious state of joy, thrilled with everything happening in his life. He had a new apartment and a new job. He was playing golf, and soon, he'd marry the woman he loved.

As winter moved in with all its fury, I was keeping warm with wedding plans—going through brides' magazines and checking out gowns, bridesmaids' dresses, and veils. I decided on colors and flowers, and I planned seating arrangements. Still, through what should have been the happiest time of my life, I was plagued by doubts. No matter how hard I tried to bury these doubts in my to-do lists—wording for the invitations, designs for centerpieces, and whether to serve fish or chicken—I couldn't shake the feeling that I simply wasn't *sure*. In the past I'd experienced sparks with guys, but no stability. Daniel offered loving stability, but where were the sparks? Had I lost my capacity to feel them?

One afternoon I was working on the guest list when my mom called. "Tina, we have a problem."

I tucked the phone under my chin as I continued to make notes in my wedding planner. "What's that?"

"These bridesmaids' dresses you've chosen. Nadine and I just went up there, and she tried hers on and it just doesn't flatter her, Tina. You need to pick something else."

"Pick something else?" I couldn't believe it. This was supposed to be my wedding and I liked those dresses.

"It's just the wrong style for her. I'm sure you can find something else that will look better on your sister."

I tossed my pen down and stood up, starting to pace as I talked. "But I like those dresses, Mom. I've built my whole wedding around those colors. You can't expect me to change everything because you don't think a dress is flattering to Nadine."

"I don't understand why you're being unreasonable about this, Tina. We can just choose another style and if it doesn't come in the same color as this one, maybe they'll have something close to it."

"Mom, I have to go. I can't talk about this right now."

Long after the phone call ended, I was still pacing around my apartment. If it hadn't been so cold, I'd have gone running, but it was early February and the wind chill was close to zero. I had to settle for pacing off my frustration, doubts, and fears.

Love. What did I even know about love? Or marriage?

Did I love Dan? How was I supposed to recognize true love? I'd had so little of it, and most of the love I experienced had either ended badly or been marred by pain.

By evening, I knew what I had to do. Go see Daniel.

By the time I got to his apartment, I was resolved. I knew I was making the right decision.

"I can't do this, Daniel." I pulled the engagement ring off my finger and set it on the coffee table. "I can't marry you."

He didn't say a word, but I could see his pain by the way he stood perfectly still, not moving a muscle.

Finally, I turned and left. I knew he was hurt, but better to end it now than hurt him worse later when everything fell apart bit by bit, as it surely would.

If I thought I was under pressure before, it was nothing compared to the pressure I felt after calling off the wedding. It was cranked up to the boiling point. First, Daniel's parents called me and asked me to dinner.

"We know how much Daniel loves you," Deborah insisted as she filled my plate. "And there's no doubt that you love him."

"There isn't?"

"Absolutely not. It's obvious to anyone who looks at you that you're in love with him. Honey, everyone gets cold feet before a wedding. Don't take it so seriously."

Okay, maybe my confusion really was just typical pre-wedding jitters. Maybe I really did love Daniel. His mother was older, wiser. Surely she knew what she was talking about.

Still, I wasn't quite ready to capitulate.

On Sunday my parents asked me to their house for dinner, and it was my mother's turn at bat. "Daniel is a good man, Tina. He loves you. And he'll never hurt you. You won't do any better than that."

"I know he loves me, Mom. That's not the question. But do I love him?"

"Of course you do. What a silly question. And you're not going to find a man who loves you as much as Daniel. You'd be foolish not to marry him."

Okay, maybe I did love him. Maybe this is what love is, a wise decision based on evidence. Surely I must be in love if everyone around me can see it so clearly. But why couldn't I be happy about it? And why couldn't I feel it?

"Okay." I took a deep breath. "Then get me married this week before I change my mind."

On Monday my mom called St. James Church and then called me in between my classes. "How about Thursday?" she asked before I barely had "hello" out of my mouth.

"How about Thursday for what?"

"Your wedding. We can get the St. James on Thursday at one."

I closed my eyes, stamping down my rising doubts. Or were those fears? "Do it."

When Daniel's parents heard about the rush wedding, they called and invited us to go with them to Las Vegas and get married there, but my mom nixed that idea right away. "You are my firstborn. I want you married here where I can attend."

And that settled that. Mom had four days to book the church, organize a reception at Lyme Stone Castle, and get me there. Getting me there may have been her biggest worry.

Monday evening she picked me up and we went over to the bridal shop where I had already ordered my dress for the June wedding. They told me there was no way they could get that dress in from the main factory and altered for me in less than two weeks. We had three days. I loved that dress, but I had to let it go. I picked out a black velvet dress with a pink sash off the rack, found one bridesmaid dress for my best friend, Rachael, and we were done.

My mom's friend started baking the wedding cake. I went on with my classes. Mom ran to the florist. And the wedding took shape, almost without my participation.

I happened to look at the calendar on Wednesday. I was getting married on Valentine's Day. A good sign!

Thursday I arrived at St. James with more butterflies in my stomach than in a field of larkspur and sweet william. There were only about twenty people there, mostly family. My mom

Tina and Dan's wedding on Valentine's Day.

Daniel and Tina on their honeymoon at Universal Studios.

took one look at my pink sash and Daniel's blue tie and shook her head. "This won't work."

She found my stepfather, who happened to be wearing a pink tie, and made him switch ties with Daniel. Then everyone gathered around us at the altar and the ceremony began.

As we stood there, my family and best friends surrounding us, I looked up at Daniel. I couldn't find a trace of doubt in his face. He knew he was doing the right thing. I wished desperately for that same assurance. Instead, I thought, *I'm going to give this two years, and if it doesn't work out in two years, I'm going to get out.*

The next morning, we flew out with Dan's parents to California. Yes, we went on our honeymoon with my new in-laws. And the truth is, we had a wonderful time. Sometimes the four of us would get together and sightsee—the Golden Gate Bridge, the Sequoia National Forest, Universal Studios, Fisherman's Wharf—and sometimes Dan and I went off alone for romantic dinners.

When we returned from our honeymoon, I moved into Dan's apartment and we set up our home.

It took me about five years, but I graduated from college and took a job working as a nutritional counselor while Daniel went from a sales job to a management position at a car dealership. I volunteered at a crisis center, but I would fall apart every time someone talked with me about his or her situation. It was taking such an emotional toll on me that I quit and went to volunteer at the Red Cross. After a while I was offered a paid position, and I couldn't have been more thrilled.

If there was a dark cloud over our marriage, it was Dan's job. Every Sunday, like clockwork, Dan would stretch out on the sofa, turn on the sports channel, and stress about going to work on Monday. He was the service manager for the dealership and took his job too much to heart. If someone came in with a complaint, he was determined to solve the problem. If they brought it back again, he owned it like a personal flaw. And Mondays were the biggest complaint days of the week.

Sunday after Sunday I watched him stress out more and more. Finally I had had enough. Pulling the coffee table closer to the sofa, I sat down, blocking Daniel's view of the football game.

"Daniel, I want you to go back to school."

Puzzled, his eyebrows knit together over his nose as he frowned. "You're blocking the television."

"I know. It was deliberate. I'm serious, Daniel. I think you should go back to school."

A flicker of impatience crossed his face. "In case you haven't noticed, Teen, I've already graduated college."

I scooted closer and touched his face. "I know—a business and marketing degree. But that's not where your heart is, Daniel. You're an engineer, just like your father. You're miserable working at the dealership, honey. Please, think about this. I know you'd be happier in mechanical engineering."

Daniel's father was an engineer and so was his brother. I'm not sure why Daniel chose business and marketing, but he was an engineer at heart, and I knew that's where he needed to be to be happy. Now, if only he could see that.

"I don't know. It's a tough business."

"Daniel, you have no idea how smart you are, do you?" I squeezed his hand. "You can do this. I have no doubts about that. You just need to recognize it for yourself."

I could tell I had him thinking, so I went off to do some housework, leaving him to ponder what I'd said and come to his own conclusion. It didn't take long.

"Okay, I'm going to do it." Daniel put his arms around me and pulled me into a hug. "But you know how tough it's going to be on you? I'm going to have school full-time and only be able to work part-time."

"I know. And it's okay. I'll be working and we'll make it.

We may have to tighten up on a few things financially, but we can make it."

And we did. I worked at the American Red Cross, and Daniel went down to Milwaukee to get his degree.

My job at the Red Cross was exciting. I was the director of Volunteer Services, coordinating disaster volunteers, recruiting them for disasters across the nation, and preparing for disaster responses. It was a great organization to work for.

Meanwhile, Daniel was busy with classes and working at the dealership on the weekends. He was right. It wasn't easy on me or on him. I missed my husband, but I knew he had to do this for himself.

Checking the finances one weekend, Daniel made a comment that caught me totally by surprise. "We're wasting our money," he announced.

I'd been working really hard to keep a tight rein on every dime we spent, so this was a shocker.

"Where?"

"The rent."

I looked around us. We had a small apartment. There were three rooms—a bathroom, a bedroom, and a space that was living room, dining room, and kitchen all in one. We could barely move without tripping over each other. How could we do better?

"We can't go smaller, Daniel."

"Not smaller, smarter."

I walked over to the dining room table and sat down next to him. "Explain this to me."

"We pay rent every month and what do we get for it?"

"A roof over our heads?"

He gave me the courtesy of a laugh, but it was brief. "Nothing, Teen. Not a dime of equity. We have about ten grand in savings. We need to take that and buy a house."

I think my jaw hit the floor, but I'm not sure. "A house? We can afford the mortgage on a house?"

He nodded and pushed his notepad closer to me. "The numbers add up. The mortgage won't be much more than we're paying now, and that includes property taxes . . . and we get a break on our income tax. We can do this."

We went house shopping right away and settled on a cute little Cape Cod starter house near the Packer Stadium. I was so excited. My first house. A home of our own!

Everything in my life was wonderful, better than I could have dreamed.

And then, out of nowhere, *he* struck again.

I had gone to my parents' house to use their computer to type some reports over the weekend. When I got there, no one was home, so I used my key, let myself in, and went to work. About half an hour later, my stepfather came in, and when I saw the look in his eye, I knew. When he reached for me, I knew. And when he pressed closer, I ran.

Shaking, I drove back home. As soon as I had the door locked behind me, I called the sexual assault center and told them what had happened. I told them everything—the sexual assault when I was five, six, seven . . . and I told them I wanted to press charges.

After asking a lot of questions, they gave me bad news. "I'm sorry, Mrs. Zahn, but the statute of limitations ran out. There's nothing we can do."

Stunned, I sat down and cried. Finally the sobs turned to sniffles, and it dawned on me that this time I could tell. I picked up the phone and called my mother. After explaining what happened, she said she'd call me back.

It was hours later before the phone rang. It was my mother. "I asked him about it, and he said he didn't touch you. He said nothing happened, that you're making this up."

My heart fell through the floor. She didn't believe me. Or didn't want to believe me.

For the first time I saw clearly through the fog of my own self-flogging over the years. The truth was shining its light on my mind. If I'd gone to my mother when the abuse started, she would not have believed me. She would not have protected me. She would have escaped into whatever story made her life easier, without regard for what her inaction might do to her daughter's heart. All the "what-ifs" that had haunted my life were squelched in that one moment of epiphany. There was nothing I could have said to my mother that would have changed my fate at the hands of my stepfather.

In the oddest way, it was an enormous relief.

chapter five

Shattered Pieces

April 1994
Green Bay, Wisconsin

I had just turned twenty-six when Daniel and I closed on our house and moved in. At school down in Milwaukee, Dan was sharing a place with three other guys and coming home on the weekends to see me and work at the dealership.

After the incident with my stepfather, I needed to be with Daniel more and more. There were times when he would pack up to go back to school on Sunday nights and I'd stand there and cry, begging him not to go, not to leave me.

Sometimes he'd relent and stay another couple of hours, but eventually he did have to go and I'd miss him terribly. I tried to bury myself in my work, but it wasn't easy. I wanted him home with me. When I turned to my family for some comfort, I was hit with another shock.

"I'm divorcing your father," my mother announced. Her call came out of the blue, and her news caught me totally off guard.

"You're doing what?"

"I said, I'm divorcing your father."

"He's not my father. He's my stepfather. And what took you so long?"

She ignored my sarcasm as she rambled on. "I've been talking to my psychiatrist about this, and he agreed that I need to get a divorce. So I talked to little Matthew and he agreed."

I wasn't sure what to say to that. Why would a grown woman ask her fourteen-year-old son if he thought it was a good idea?

"I'm going to have him served at Kmart."

Now she had my full attention. "Kmart? What's with that?"

"He's been really abusive lately, and I don't want him in the house when I tell him. I'm going to call and tell him I need him to come up to Kmart to help me, and when he gets there, he'll be served."

I wasn't sure it would work, but all I could do was pray that my stepfather was going to be reasonable when he was served with the divorce papers.

My brother Kyle called me a couple hours later. "Did you hear what happened?"

"Just that Mom called to say she was serving our stepfather with divorce papers today."

Kyle snorted. "Yeah, she did that. And the man went ballistic.

He actually came in where I was working and started screaming right in the middle of the place, accusing me of knowing
and not warning him ahead of time."

I sat down on the edge of the waterbed, trying to picture poor
Kyle having to deal with my angry stepfather at his job.

"Lucky for me, there was an off-duty police officer there and
she escorted him out. The boss let me off, so I followed him
to the house. Did you know Mom already packed all his stuff
and put it out in the van?"

"Oh, no! He must have been furious."

"Worse," Kyle told me. "He wanted to get in the house to get
his gun, but Mom had the house all locked up so he couldn't
get in. Tina, he was talking all suicidal, so they took him to
Brown County Mental Health Institute."

When Daniel came home from school, I told him what had
happened.

"I think we should go visit him in the hospital."

All I could do was stare at the man I married. Go visit the
man that molested me? "Not on your life, Daniel. I can't believe
you're even suggesting it."

He shrugged. "I'll ask my dad to go with me. Your stepfather
just had everything in his life ripped out from under him. He
needs to know someone in this world cares."

There was no point in arguing with Dan about this, so I let
him go. The truth was I knew my stepfather had Daniel fooled,
just the way he fooled everyone. To the world my stepfather
was a good, kind, devoted family man. But those of us who
grew up around him knew better. He was angry, abusive, and

violent. And for Daniel to go visit him was like saying that the sexual abuse I suffered meant nothing.

I don't know what Daniel said to my stepfather during their visit, and I didn't ask. Daniel and I had discussed my stepfather's abuse a few times, and he just didn't seem to understand how deeply I was affected—maybe because when he met me, I appeared to be on good terms with the man. Anyway, I knew it was futile to argue with my husband about it. All I could do was hope that eventually he'd come to understand what had been done to me.

My parents' divorce changed my mother dramatically. Suddenly it seemed as though she didn't want to have anything to do with her three older children. It was bad enough that Daniel was gone all week at school, but now my mother was essentially gone as well. I'd call her and make plans to see her for dinner or lunch, and at the last minute she'd cancel—or not show up at all. At first I didn't understand, but then Kyle let me know it was because our mom had a new boyfriend.

We were not only stunned, we were hurt. Then Mom told us she was selling the house on Robin Avenue. Suddenly the house we grew up in was gone and Mom had disappeared from our lives. Daniel was away at school. I felt totally abandoned. It was just too much damage to my life—like a tornado had ripped through and all the security I thought I'd built was little more than shattered pieces on the ground.

It was about then that a girlfriend of mine suggested that I come to work with her at a trucking company in Green Bay. I guess I was just looking for a new challenge, so I gave up my job at the Red Cross and went to work with Cathy.

I was excited about the position at first. The company was one of the largest in the country and offered an on-site health club, a cafeteria, excellent health benefits, and good pay. But sitting behind a desk all day grew old quickly.

A few months into the job, I started experiencing severe pain, first in my arms and hands, and then in my shoulders. One day, I turned around to speak to someone and a pain rushed up my arms and across my back like a fire. Within minutes, I was unable to type.

The company sent me to a doctor, and I was diagnosed with nerve damage. The more I used my arms, the worse the pain would get. It was difficult to do the simplest things—peeling a potato, brushing my hair, getting dressed.

To encourage me to keep fighting, Daniel bought me a Precious Moments figurine of a little soldier in full armor. And I did have a fight on my hands. The trucking company was refusing to pay the medical bills, so we ended up in arbitration.

When I was feeling adrift and without family, Daniel's mother, Deborah, stepped in and tried to bring me closer to the Zahn family. My friend Rachael did the same, inviting me to her family events, but I was so afraid of rejection that I couldn't be myself around any of them. I wore a mask, pretending to be the person I believed they wanted and expected me to be. I told them what they wanted to hear, went along with whatever they planned, and swallowed whatever objections I had.

Daniel's family had been attending St. Paul Lutheran Church while Dan and I had been attending St. James, but now, when Deborah suggested that Daniel and I attend St. Paul with her and Daniel's father, I compliantly went along with the suggestion, even though I didn't want to attend there and didn't feel I was being fed spiritually at that church. But I was so afraid that if I didn't do what they wanted, I would be rejected. I just couldn't face that again.

I couldn't emotionally deal with one more person tossing me aside for not living up to their expectations.

One afternoon, I decided to drive from my home in Green Bay up to my mom's new house in Shawano in the hope of seeing her and perhaps making some emotional connection. Instead, I found the house in an uproar.

Mom was in the kitchen, emptying the dishwasher, when I came through the door. "Hi, Mom."

She looked up at me and I could see the anger in her face. Immediately, old fears sliced through me, and I had to remind myself that she couldn't be mad at me.

"You might want to talk to your sister," she hissed through clenched teeth. "I'm done trying to get through to her. If she wants to act like a fool, who am I to stop her?"

"Whitney?"

She slammed the cabinet door closed. "No, Nadine. She's pregnant."

"Pregnant?" I slipped my jacket off and draped it over the back of the kitchen chair.

"And she can't decide what she wants to do. All she does is stay curled up in her bed, acting like the world has come to an end."

"I'll go talk to her," I said softly as I left the kitchen.

Nadine was half asleep when I slipped into the room. "Nadine?"

"Hmmm?"

"I thought we might talk."

She kicked back the covers and sat up, running her fingers through her hair. "I don't know why. You can't possibly understand what I'm going through."

I sat down on the edge of the bed. "Oh, I understand better than you think. I got pregnant when I was dating Terry."

Nadine's eyes widened as she pulled her knees to her chest and wrapped her arms around them. "I never knew that."

"I never told anyone."

"Then you had an abortion?"

"Two of them," I whispered.

"Mom wants me to have an abortion, but I don't want that, Tina. I'm so confused."

"What does the father have to say about the baby?" I scooted up further on the bed, tucking one leg under me.

"He wants the baby and he wants to marry me, but he said he'd respect whatever decision I made."

"Do you want to marry him?"

Nadine shrugged. "I don't know for sure. I mean, I love him, but I'm just not sure about marriage yet."

I took a deep breath. "I'm not going to tell you what to do.

You have to make that decision for yourself, but I want you to know what you're facing if you decide on an abortion."

For the next half hour, I told her all about my horrific experiences—the cold, clinical procedure, the indifferent medical staff, the nightmarish sounds of the vacuum, the pain after the anesthesia wore off, and then the pain in my heart as I recuperated, a pain that has never quite gone away.

"And Mom wants me to go through that?" Nadine shook her head. "How could she even suggest it?"

"Maybe she doesn't know what it's really like. Some people seem to think it's no big deal—just some tissue that needs to be removed, but it's not, Nadine. It's a child with a beating heart."

"Well, the only reason I was even considering abortion was because Mom was putting pressure on me, but after hearing what you went through. . . . No way am I going to go through that. I want this baby."

She crawled over me to reach the phone. As she dialed, I closed my eyes and took a deep breath. I knew she was making the right decision. No one should have to live with the pain I'd been living with.

"It's me. I'm keeping the baby. And I'm willing to talk marriage."

I slid off the bed and left her to make plans with the baby's father. Mom was at the front door, putting lipstick on in front of the mirror, as I came out of Nadine's room. She twisted the lipstick closed and dropped it in her purse. "Is she going to have the abortion?"

Shaking my head, I went into the kitchen and picked up my

jacket. She followed right behind me. "What! What did you tell her? She's going to ruin her life having this baby."

"Mom." I took another deep breath, preparing myself for the onslaught of her temper. "If she gets an abortion, she'll regret it the rest of her life. I didn't tell her what to do. I only told her what one option meant. The decision was hers to make and she made it."

"And how would you know she'll regret an abortion?"

Looking over my shoulder, I opened the back door. "Because I regret both of my abortions with every fiber of my being."

Shocked speechless, she stared at me with wide eyes. Taking advantage of the silence, I walked out the door and closed it behind me.

chapter six

Depression's Foothold

May 1995
Green Bay, Wisconsin

After a long and taxing court case, the judge finally handed down a settlement decision on the arbitration between the trucking company and me. Immediately after the settlement, I left the company and went to work for the American Diabetes Association. I had my office in Green Bay, but since the main office was in Virginia, I was the only one in this office. As the director for the northeast Wisconsin area, I was in charge of fund-raisers, getting a board of directors up and running in the area, setting up programs, and scheduling events. I was constantly on the road, traveling from one luncheon or meeting to another.

The more there was to do, the more I did. I buried myself

in my work, keeping long hours—my husband was away at school, so there was no one waiting at home for me anyway. I was constantly working harder and harder, trying to be perfect, trying to be the best director they'd ever had.

The stress finally caught up with me, and I started having anxiety attacks. Because of the severity of these attacks, I went to the doctor. He did some tests and put me on some medication to slow my heart down, but when I took it, I felt so tired I had trouble getting everything done that I needed to do, so I stopped taking the medication.

Then one day, walking up a flight of stairs, I heard something in my heart pop. My heart felt as if it were swallowing itself—and it's never been the same since. I was diagnosed with super ventricular tachycardia, which means that, in an unpredictable way, my heart sometimes speeds up disproportionately to my activity level. From that point on, to preserve my health, I had to be more careful with taking on stress.

In addition to heart problems, I was still in tremendous pain from the injury at the trucking company. Many days I'd have to go home and lie down for an hour to get through the worst of the pain.

January 28, 1996
Super Bowl Sunday
Green Bay, Wisconsin

The Dallas Cowboys were taking on the Pittsburgh Steelers in Arizona for the big game of the year. We were disappointed that our beloved Packers weren't in the Super Bowl. They had made it to the playoffs but lost against the Carolina Panthers a few weeks earlier.

Still, the Super Bowl is a big thing in football towns, and Green Bay is no exception. The town celebrates whether the Packers are in the game or not.

Daniel and I arrived at his parents' house about the same time as his cousin Joel got there. We all walked in together, looking forward to the great food Deborah would have prepared. This year, Daniel's brother, Michael, was in Germany and unable to attend the traditional family gathering.

Greatgram, Daniel's grandmother, was helping Deborah in the kitchen. I noticed Deborah looked a little pale, but I dismissed it as fatigue since she was working three part-time jobs. But within a few minutes, Deborah leaned against the counter. "I need to lie down."

Greatgram and I finished up the food and then we all watched the game. Dan's dad, Howard, went to check on Deborah at one point and said she was asleep. She slept through the entire game, so no one bothered to wake her to say good-bye when we all left.

Daniel and I were barely in our house when the phone rang. It was Howard.

"Tina, where's Daniel?"

"He's closing up the garage, Howard." I could hear the terror in his voice. "What's wrong?"

"Deborah. They've taken her."

He wasn't making any sense, his words running together

as he panted into the phone. "Who has taken her, Howard? What's wrong?"

At that moment, Daniel entered the bedroom. Hearing my tone of voice was enough for him to realize there was an emergency. He held out his hand for the phone.

In a few minutes he'd calmed his dad, understood what had transpired, and promised to come right away. Pale and shaken, he hung up the phone.

"What's going on?" I asked him.

"Dad said he tried to wake Mom up after we left and couldn't." Looking around the room in a panic he asked, "Where's my jacket?"

"You probably hung it on a kitchen chair," I said, still not comprehending what was happening.

Daniel rushed out of the bedroom and I followed him. He slipped on his jacket. "Mom wouldn't wake up, and she was making this weird kind of snoring noise, so Dad called 911." He stared at me blankly. "Get your coat. We have to go, honey."

"Go where?" I nearly screamed, trying to make sense of all the panic.

"To the hospital! Dad says it looks bad. They've taken her to Saint Vincent's Hospital."

I grabbed my coat out of the closet and my purse off the table and was out the door and in the car before Daniel had a chance to get it started. He and I rushed to the hospital, arriving just as the doctor was coming out to speak to Howard.

"I'm sorry, but I don't think your wife is going to make it through the night. She's suffered a severe stroke, a cerebral hemorrhage." It took a couple minutes for the words to sink in. How could she die? She didn't even have her grandchildren yet. Her mother was still alive. She wasn't old enough to die. How could this be happening?

When the doctor finished explaining the situation, he left. For a few moments, all we could do was stand there. We tried to comfort each other with one thought—she wasn't gone yet.

Howard asked the doctor to call in a neurosurgeon. Daniel called Michael in Germany and told him to take the first flight home.

Then in the midst of the heavy silence, Howard turned and touched my shoulder. I could feel the weight of his fear as he spoke. "Would you mind going and picking up Greatgram? I've put off calling her until I knew how serious this was, but she needs to be told and she'll want to come."

"I'll go get her. Don't worry about that." I gave him a hug and hurried to the parking lot.

Greatgram lived just a mile away from the hospital, but I think it was the longest mile I've ever driven. My foot was shaking so much I could barely keep it steady on the gas pedal.

"God, you can't take her yet. She can't go yet. We didn't even have kids yet, and she wants grandkids. She can't go yet."

The prayer kept rolling off my lips, over and over, until I pulled into Greatgram's driveway. After I rang the doorbell, it took her a few minutes to get to the door. As I waited, trying to be calm, I rehearsed what I had to say.

How do you tell someone her daughter could be dying?

Greatgram wasn't young, and she shouldn't be burying her own daughter. She shouldn't even have to consider such a thing.

Finally Greatgram opened the door, sleepy-eyed in her pajamas.

"Tina?" she mumbled.

"Greatgram, I need you to get dressed. We have to go to the hospital. It's Deborah. She . . . she had a stroke, Greatgram. It's not good." I stepped in and shut the door behind me.

"Stroke? Deborah? Oh, my." She stumbled backward as if physically struck by my words.

"I'm here to take you to the hospital. You need to get dressed."

She stared at me, a vacant look in her eyes. "Dressed?"

Overwhelmed by the news about her daughter, she was having trouble focusing. I helped her get dressed, and we hurried out the door.

When Greatgram and I arrived back at the hospital, the neurosurgeon had been called in and there was nothing to do but wait. And pray. At one point Greatgram turned to us and said quietly, "I think we need to pray the Lord's Prayer."

Deborah made it through the night. In fact, she recovered completely, but it was a long recovery and she lost large segments of her memory. After Deborah was released from the hospital, Greatgram went over and took care of her during the day while Howard was at work.

When Deborah was strong enough to go out on her own, she found that she had forgotten how to drive, forgotten where certain parts of the city were, and forgotten how to get from one location to another.

Greatgram was a strong woman, still living on her own, still driving, still running all her errands for herself, and still pitching in to help others in need. Those wonderful qualities were a gift to her daughter all over again. The woman who had once taught Deborah to walk and talk as a little girl was now encouraging her middle-aged child to learn basic living skills. Deborah needed every ounce of her mother's strength, fortitude, and can-do personality.

Four months after Deborah's stroke, Daniel graduated with his engineering degree. As he was wont to do, Daniel went off to play golf one afternoon and met a man named Bob. As they talked over a game of golf, Daniel discussed his recent graduation and Bob talked about his company. By the end of the game, Bob had hired Daniel to come work for him.

With Daniel settled into his new job and my job at American Diabetes secure, we decided it was time for the next phase of our lives. We started planning our family and looking for a bigger house. We searched all over the Green Bay area but nothing was quite what we wanted. So, after much discussion, we decided to buy a lot and build exactly what we wanted. We found two lots. Both were a nice size, bordered by woods in the back, in new developments, and convenient to Daniel's office. One was just a mile from Daniel's parents and the other was just a quarter mile from my friend Rachael.

Naturally, Daniel's parents voted for the one closest to them, but Daniel and I ended up buying the lot near Rachael. Part of the reason we chose this lot was that, as much as I loved Deborah, she had become far more involved in our lives than I wanted. After her stroke she'd been unable to go back to work, which left her with lots of time to occupy. Our choice of a lot was a tough decision. On the one hand, I desperately wanted Deborah's approval and love, but on the other hand, I needed my space.

We bought the lot and met with the contractors. There was only one detail about the house that I wouldn't compromise on—*no basement*. Daniel worked around that by having the contractor add to the finished lower level huge bay windows that overlooked the woods in the back.

We had no idea that building our own home would be as complicated and as demanding as it was. We had to choose cabinets, floors, windows, paint, tile, carpeting, doorknobs, bath fixtures—it was an endless cycle of running to meet the contractor, running to look at samples, running to stores to look at products. Before long, I was worn out.

Being so tired and experiencing a feeling that was oddly familiar, I did a test, and sure enough, I was pregnant.

As excited as we were at the prospect of our first child, it was definitely the wrong time in regard to the demands on our time. I had so little energy that I could barely make it through a meeting without falling asleep in my chair.

As our new house grew closer to being finished, there was the additional responsibility of prepping our Cape Cod to put it on the market, then the open houses, the Realtors in and out, the constant struggle to keep everything perfect, never knowing when someone would want to see it.

Feeling overwhelmed was starting to be familiar.

June 1998
Green Bay, Wisconsin

Our dream home was almost done. The contractors were promising us that we could take possession in about six weeks. I was nine months pregnant and struggling to stay on top of all the details for the new house and oversee the beginning stages of packing up the Cape Cod. I knew I wouldn't be able to get much packing done after the baby was born, so I was trying to accomplish as much as I could beforehand.

I packed boxes, rested, folded clothes, rested, wrapped dishes, rested, sorted through books, and rested some more. It never seemed to be enough. However, just before I went into labor, I felt rejuvenated, energized, and alert. I'd read all the *What to Expect When You Are Expecting* books. I knew I was in "nesting mode," which meant the baby was coming. When I felt the first contraction I wasn't surprised, but I wanted to make sure this was real labor and not the Braxton Hicks contractions that fooled so many women into going to the hospital only to be turned away with the diagnosis of "false labor."

Thunder rumbled the skies and rain fell in torrents. It was one of those days when you curl up with a good book and a cup of hot tea, glad you don't have to be out in the storm. I wasn't curled up with a book, of course. I had too much to do. I'd been having contractions on and off all day, but I was thrilled to be inside as lightning flashed and crackled, filling the air with expectancy.

Suddenly I felt another contraction; this one was hard enough to make me double over. "Dan," I called weakly.

Daniel was unaware of what was happening. He was busy taping a box shut and said, "I think I found a way for us to save some money on this move."

"Daniel!"

His head came up fast. "Teen?"

"Now!"

"Are you sure?"

I'd been having contractions for hours. I was sure.

Like the classic cliché opening to a novel, it was a dark and stormy night, June 25, 1998, when our daughter, Sarah, made her debut. While lightning and thunder held most people's attention, Daniel and I couldn't take our eyes off this beautiful child. She was the most precious thing I'd ever held or even seen—and she was mine. I could barely stand to be apart from her for her checkups, counting the minutes until the nurse brought her back to me.

Daniel's mother was as enthralled as I was. After two sons, she finally had a little girl to fuss over and spoil.

A few days later Daniel brought us home, and suddenly there weren't enough hours in a day to get everything done—caring for Sarah, getting used to being a new mother, overseeing the finishing touches on the new house, shopping, laundry, packing, cleaning, and meeting with the contractors. The days blended into weeks and before I knew it, moving day had arrived. Or should I say, moving *days*.

I stood up, bracing my hand on my lower back and stretching the kink out. "Tell me again why we didn't just rent a big truck to do it all in one day."

"It's cheaper doing it a little at a time." Daniel picked up the box and stacked it in the corner of the dining room. "It'll be fine. You'll see."

He thought this was all going well. I, on the other hand, felt frustrated from start to finish. We had made so many trips I lost count, and everything seemed so disorganized. I was constantly sick to my stomach, tired, unable to sleep, and barely able to find the strength to feed Sarah. I just wanted to curl up in bed, pull the comforter over my face, and not come out until the house was all set up, everything unpacked and put away, and dinner ready.

Sarah's whimper reminded me why I couldn't do that. Walking over to her cradle, I picked her up and touched her silky soft cheek with my finger. "Hungry again, Sarah?"

Just then Dan called, "Tina, did you call about getting the water turned on at the new house?"

Sighing heavily, I carried Sarah through the maze of boxes to find a chair to sit in so that I could feed her. "Yes, Daniel."

"Did you call everyone about the party to welcome Sarah?"

"No." I dropped a soft kiss on Sarah's forehead. "I made it

through half the list, and then the contractor called about the flooring in the master bath and I never did get back to it."

There were so many details, details, details. I could never catch up. I neglected many important things as each day brought a new batch of pressing matters. There were so many tasks to accomplish that the importance of my feeling better was overwhelmed by the growing to-do lists.

One day the doorbell rang, and before Daniel and I could decide who was going to answer it, it eased open and Daniel's father stuck his head in. "Busy?"

"Hey, Dad!" Daniel set his tape gun down on the box he was sealing. "Come to help pack?"

"I can, but I actually came bearing gifts."

Dan had to help Howard and Deborah carry the box in, and as soon as I saw what was in it, my heart sank. It was a Jenny Lind crib. It was a wonderful gift, but there was one problem. I didn't want a Jenny Lind crib and I didn't want a crib in dark wood. I had already picked out the one I wanted for Sarah—a sleigh-bed crib in light oak.

"We found it at a yard sale and it only cost us eighty bucks!" Howard was saying as he started pulling out the pieces.

"A bargain," Deborah added with a huge smile. She was so excited, you could almost see her vibrating with joy. "It's just like the crib we had for Daniel and Michael when they were babies. Don't you just love it, Tina?"

I forced myself to smile. "Sure. It's beautiful."

And it was. It just wasn't what I wanted for Sarah.

Right after we finished moving into the new house, we

had the party for Sarah. The familiar fatigue fell over me like a heavy tent. I could barely get through the day. On top of the usual back pain, I had a stomachache that lasted all day. Someone must have noticed how tired I was because the guests all left early, and I barely had the energy to climb into bed.

Daniel started getting up in the middle of the night to feed Sarah while I slept. My back pain was so severe it made it difficult to care for Sarah during the day. Daniel's parents were around to help out, but their help, while greatly appreciated, still felt like interference and made me feel resentful.

Deborah and Greatgram would show up with clothes for Sarah that they picked up from yard sales, thrift shops, and clothing stores. They filled her closet and dresser with outfits that, while nice, weren't what I would have bought for her.

Howard showed up to hang the Raggedy Anne valance in the nursery, while Deborah placed the new Raggedy Anne comforter in the Jenny Lind crib. I watched and smiled and all the while wanted white lace and satin with pink trim.

Finally, it all built up until I couldn't keep silent any longer. One night I expressed my feelings to Daniel. His response surprised me.

"Teen, it's Mom's first granddaughter; let her do this for Sarah. What's the big deal?"

The big deal was that while Sarah might be Deborah's first granddaughter, she was my first daughter and I had no say in what she wore, how the nursery was decorated, or what kind of crib she slept in.

And it hurt that Daniel would put his mother's feelings before mine.

Wounded, I retreated back into my realm of silence and fatigue. I said little, did less, and slept more.

All of the little things had added up to something more overwhelming than I could have predicted. Each incident, taken by itself, was no big deal. But I wasn't able to let things roll off my back. Had I been more emotionally strong, I would have spoken up for myself, kindly but firmly. Instead, I let the boundaries in my life become blurred, too tired to sort it all out, too weak to defend my feelings. After all, Dan and his family were such nice people. They meant well. So my feelings went the path of least resistance; they were pushed down, stuffed, and ignored.

The only problem with this method of dealing with inner conflict is that your physical body doesn't seem to accept the plan.

I went back to work when Sarah was twelve weeks old. I was still having stomachaches, and with the additional stress of being back on the job, it wasn't unusual for me to stop and throw up on my way to work. Finally I went to the doctor, and he diagnosed postpartum depression. After giving me a prescription for Prozac, he assured me that I'd be feeling like my old self in no time.

In spite of his optimistic prognosis, it took nearly a year for me to bounce back even a little from the depression. The problem was, between all the fund-raisers, volunteer meetings, traveling, and nights working, I was getting burned out. Having to run home and take care of Sarah, make dinner, throw laundry in the washer, and straighten up the house just was more than I could handle, and I knew something had to change.

One of my friends told me about a part-time position as a pharmaceutical rep. I'd have no benefits, but I would make the same money and have to work only three days a week. I could even choose which days to work. It sounded too good to be true. I applied for the job, was hired, and gave my notice at the American Diabetes Association.

You know what they say about things that sound too good to be true. Sure enough, three weeks into the job, the employees were told that the contract had run out and we were all being let go. I couldn't believe they hired us and didn't tell us beforehand that it was only temporary, but it was too late to argue the point. I had to find another job fast.

I found one at Bristol Meyers Squibb as a rep working with antibiotics and anti-anxiety medications, but I had to go back to working full time. Daniel and I talked it over. The job meant more hours, but it also provided great benefits and a company car. Daniel felt I should take the position, so I accepted the job and flew to New Jersey for training.

I felt sorry for my roommate during the training. It was stressful enough to be rushed through this intensive training, but then she had to put up with the fact that if she slipped into the room after I had gone to sleep, I would start screaming at the top of my lungs until I woke up and realized what was happening. For years I had struggled with this problem, but nothing seemed to help. Daniel finally learned that if I went to bed first, he needed to walk into the room talking. That would wake me up before I had a chance to sense a presence in the darkness. My roommate, on the other hand, wasn't as patient as Daniel and made her opinions known quite clearly.

When I finished training and returned home, I was given a huge territory to cover that included Green Bay and everything north into Michigan and the Upper Peninsula. This meant being away from home five or six nights a month.

The only bright spot at the time was that my mother finally broke up with the man she was seeing and started dating a man down in Appleton. We were so thrilled that all of us attended Christmas dinner at his house to show our mother some support.

In the meantime, traveling with the job was getting old. I was doing an oil change a month, was away from home far too much, and was missing my daughter when we were apart.

I heard about another pharmaceutical company that had a smaller territory available with no overnight traveling. Regulations require a foreign company to partner with an American company to release a new drug here in the United States. In this instance, a Japanese company was releasing a new cholesterol medication, so they linked with Parke Davis to form Sankyo Parke Davis. In this new job, I set off to present the new medication to doctors in the region, wondering why they couldn't come up with some new miracle drug to make me feel happy.

chapter seven

Changes in the Wind

September 11, 2001
Green Bay, Wisconsin

S tanding in line at Festival Foods, I double-checked my shopping list. I was hosting a luncheon for a group of doctors at a clinic in Two Rivers and wanted to make sure everything was perfect.

After a short time with Sankyo Parke Davis, I had gone back to work for Bristol Meyers. I still had the travel and the nights away, but it wasn't nearly as stressful as Sankyo had turned out to be. Because of the push to make sales and earn commissions, a sales position in any field is going to be stressful, but working for Sankyo when they were launching a new product pushed the stress levels over the top, as we were pressured to get the new drug introduced and sold in the marketplace.

"Did you hear what happened?" a man in line behind me said to someone.

"No, what?" a woman responded.

"A plane just crashed into the Twin Towers in New York. I just heard it on the radio."

My shopping list forgotten, I jumped into the conversation. "A plane?"

The man nodded at me. "That's what they said—a commercial airliner."

It was beautiful day in Green Bay—brilliant blue skies with barely a cloud to mar the color. I had no idea what the weather was like in New York City, but didn't they have computers to keep planes from running into buildings if visibility was bad? Thoughts raced through my head as I checked out and hurried to my car.

As soon as I had the groceries in the trunk, I got behind the wheel and turned on the radio, anxious for more details. A second plane had struck, this time hitting the other tower. Terrorists, they thought, with perhaps more than forty thousand people dead.

My heart was racing and my hands shaking as I listened to the news all the way to Twin Rivers. Another plane hit the Pentagon. Another went down in a field in Pennsylvania. Our country was under attack.

I felt sick to my stomach.

As soon as I arrived at the clinic, I grabbed my supplies and rushed inside. The clinic had their television on and everyone had their eyes glued to the news.

"Did you hear?" someone asked me as soon as I came through the door.

"I heard on the radio."

Just then they showed a replay of the planes hitting the Twin Towers, and my mind could not accept what my eyes were seeing.

"I don't believe it," I said softly, setting my bags down on the counter.

One nurse had tears tracking through her mascara, leaving ugly black streaks on her heavily rouged cheeks. She hitched back a sob. "This is just horrible."

While I prepared and served the lunch, we watched the towers fall over and over and over—each time thinking that this time we'd move from disbelief to acceptance, but it never happened.

After the luncheon I hurried home and turned on the news to continue watching. It was too surreal, too far-fetched. America? Under attack? Terrorists on our soil? Was this how people felt when Pearl Harbor had been attacked? Did they feel the same shock, disbelief, and fear?

Daniel came home from work and joined me in front of the television. We watched until late into the night, each trying to come to terms with what was happening, grieving for all those who were never coming home, crying for those wandering the streets trying to find their relatives and friends, angry at the senseless murder of so many innocent people.

When I woke up the next morning, it was cloudy and overcast, but I barely noticed as I rushed to turn on the news.

Relieved that there had been no further attacks overnight, I sat down in the kitchen and cried as I watched the reporters interviewing one person after another, each holding up a picture of someone they loved and couldn't find.

What if I didn't come home tonight? What if Daniel went to work this morning and I never saw him again? How do you cope with the sudden loss? You kiss someone good-bye in the morning, assuming you'll see him or her again at dinner, and you don't. You never see your loved one again.

Life is too precious and too short to be wasted. I asked myself what we were doing with our lives. I was working a job, but it wasn't my passion. I made good money, but I was missing so much of Sarah's life. Was this the way it was supposed to be? I was missing my child's first attempt to sing a song or read a book because I had to make a sale or because I wanted to have the best sales record of the month. What did that bring in the end?

For hours I sat and questioned every aspect of my life and finally realized what the reward had been for staying busy: a hole in my empty heart.

In the days following the attacks, I drove off to work, wondering how to fill that hole. Not surprisingly I found no answers. Months slipped by and winter arrived with all its fury. Still nothing. I realized that depression had become a way of life for me. I saw no way out. I just kept putting one foot in front of the other.

Driving up the highway, heading back into the outer reaches of Michigan, I stared at the road ahead of me and felt awash with futility. "I don't know how much longer I can handle this," I whispered.

March 2002
Green Bay, Wisconsin

I had the best sales of any region and had just won a trip to Disney World for my entire family, so I couldn't imagine why my manager was calling me. I took a deep breath, waiting for her to tell me what was on her mind. My thoughts raced through one scenario after another. Could it be a promotion, a demotion, a different territory, more money?

Finally, she got to the point of the conversation. "This isn't easy for me, Tina. You're one of the top sales reps in the country, but I have to let you go."

Of all the scenarios I'd played out, this wasn't even on my list. "Let me go? But why?"

"It's not personal. I have to let everyone go." I could hear her tapping something nervously on her desk. "I had no idea, Tina. This was as much a surprise to me as it is to you. There's nothing I can do."

Stunned, I got off the phone and walked into my kitchen. They had fired everyone. The entire sales force was gone in one fell swoop. That's why the big push recently to increase sales. That's why the big promotion to win a trip for four to Disney World. *That's why the pressure had been on.* To get everything sold before everyone was laid off.

Numb, I wandered from one spot to another. I'd worked

myself to the point of exhaustion for this company, given up time with my baby and my family, stayed night after night in some motel in the middle of Michigan, all to give this company my best, and this is how they treated me. I'd worked in spite of the extreme pain I was suffering in my back and arms. I worked in spite of the severe depression. I worked when I'd rather have been home with my baby. I worked when I was sick and when I was tired. And now, without warning, I'd been laid off.

I walked to the window and stared out into the woods behind our house. "Okay, God, what's next?"

I didn't expect an answer, of course. It wasn't that I didn't believe in God—I did. It's just that he hadn't exactly been the central focus of my life. Daniel and I attended church—the Lutheran church that he'd grown up in and that his parents still attended—but it had never grabbed me by the heart and changed my life. My belief system, however, included prayer, and therefore it was not unusual for me to pray to God.

But this particular morning, as soon as I said, "Okay, God, what's next?" I thought about Green Bay Community Church. Whitney had been attending there, as well as one of my closest friends. Both had been inviting me to attend for some time, but I'd never given it a second thought. I had a church. Why did I need another one? I had to stop and think. I had been attending Dan's parents' church for years but still didn't feel that I was being served spiritually. If anything, I felt like my relationship with God was going backward. Could that be why I felt so empty inside? It was worth checking out my sister's church. I was at loose ends and needed something. It couldn't hurt to find out if the answers were waiting for me there.

I called my sister and told her I was going to attend her church.

On Sunday morning, I put Sarah in children's church and went into the service with my sister. I wasn't sure what to expect, but what awaited me blew every expectation I had right out the window.

The building was a multifunctional building that was used for various events from plays and church to basketball games and meetings. Most churches sit empty during much of the week, and that has always seemed like such a waste to me. Here was a church that truly reached out and became a part of the community. I liked that.

More than half of the congregation had left traditional churches, and the remainder came from various other denominations. Everything was so laid back, right down to the coffee shop where you could get something to drink and take it into the service with you.

The next thing that struck me was the music. I had no idea that music like this existed. Instead of the tried and true old hymns out of a book, this church had a band that sang contemporary songs. The first song they sang was one called "Awesome God," and it was like suddenly I saw God in a whole new way, a way I could relate to, a way I could understand.

Then the pastor's message blew me away as well. It was so relevant to where I was in my life that I felt as if God had reached down through the heavens and touched me.

At the end of the service, the pastor stepped forward and explained that the first step to having a relationship with the Lord is to simply acknowledge that you need him, that you can't do it alone, that no matter how hard you try to be a good person, it is never enough, and that you want him to step into your life and guide you.

I felt every word pull on my heart, and I needed to be closer to this God who loves me, to explore this unconditional love, and to know him in a way I'd never imagined possible. I wanted to have this personal relationship with God.

When the pastor led us in a prayer to invite the Lord into our lives, I prayed it with all my heart.

I floated out of the church that morning, realizing that this was what I'd been missing.

"No, that is *not* a church. A building with pews and an altar and a cross and stained glass—that's a church!" Daniel slammed the car door and shoved the key into the ignition.

"It *is* a church! They worship God in there. What more does a church need?"

I'd asked Daniel to attend Green Bay Community Church with me, and I'd been so sure he was going to see what I saw—feel what I felt. I couldn't have been more wrong. He hadn't liked a single thing about it.

Crushed, I sat there and stared out the window as we drove home in near silence. The only one who seemed to feel like talking was Sarah, rattling on from the backseat about what she had learned in children's church.

When Daniel's parents and grandmother stopped over later in the day, the battle began again.

"I know someone who goes to that church," Greatgram interjected as I tried to explain what I liked about it. "She was always pushing me and pushing me to go there. It was like an obsession with her or something, like I'm not a Christian if I don't attend there."

Deborah nodded in total agreement. "She did the same to me. It made me so uncomfortable. I just know it's a cult."

"It's *not* a cult!" Why couldn't I make them understand?

"I don't know if it's really a cult or not." Daniel shoved back from the table and headed for the refrigerator. "But I can tell you it's not a church. Where are their core beliefs? The Lutherans, the Methodists, the Presbyterians—they have core beliefs. What are these people's core beliefs?"

I could only stare at my hands clasped in front of me on the table as Daniel and his family continued to condemn what I had found to be the source of such joy. I'm sure they were all trying to be helpful, but it felt as if they were ganging up on me, forcing me to bend back to their way, their church, their idea of what I should be. When was someone going to love me for who I was and accept the choices I made for myself?

The next morning I made a point of going to the nearest Christian bookstore and buying a couple of CDs of some new worship music. I found a radio station that broadcast sermons from some of the more popular pastors across the country and played upbeat, uplifting worship music. It was so invigorating and stimulating, I kept it on most of the day.

During the week, things appeared normal on the surface, but on Sunday mornings, the tension was manifested in a battle of wills. Daniel would insist on attending the Lutheran church, while I insisted on attending Green Bay Community Church.

My relationship with God became almost secretive. Daniel would go off to work in the morning, Sarah would go to pre-school, and I would sit down and work my way through an online Bible study by Beth Moore, a popular teacher and best-selling author. No one knew, and I wasn't going to tell them. It would just give them one more thing to push me not to do.

I became more and more involved with Green Bay Community Church—women's ministry, children's church, and then MOPS (Mothers of Preschoolers). It opened up a whole new world for me as I found a place where I felt safe, where I *belonged*.

And then came a Sunday morning that changed my life again, opening up a whole new way of thinking.

The youth pastor would occasionally preach on Sunday mornings, and when he did it was always wonderful. He stood somewhere around six feet, four inches and would take these long strides from one end of the platform to the other while he spoke, keeping everyone's eyes glued to him as they took in every word.

"... and since I couldn't sleep, I got up out of bed and went to sit in my den for a little while. I sat there on my sofa and talked to God for well over an hour, explaining to him ..."

His words ran over me like warm oil, saturating every thought. *Sit and talk to God? Explain to him? Just talk to him?* I couldn't believe what I was hearing. No one had ever talked like this in any church I'd ever been in. But the prospect of being able to just talk to God anytime, anywhere—now that was exciting.

That night after everyone had gone to bed, I went into my living room, curled up on the sofa, and after a few halting starts and stops, began to just talk to the Lord. It was awkward at first, but soon I felt his presence and his peace in a way I'd never thought possible. Why hadn't someone told me about this years ago?

From that moment on, my prayer life took on a vibrancy and depth all its own. It was like suddenly finding a hidden treasure of untold wealth right in your own backyard after years of poverty.

Daniel and I discussed my going back to work, but I wanted to stay at home with Sarah. I was having fun, spending time with my daughter, the church, women's ministry, a summer book club, MOPS, the Bible study, and women's retreats—although I didn't give him all those reasons for wanting to stay home. Since he was doing well enough at work that we could afford it, he agreed that I could be a stay-at-home mom.

My days were full and my heart fuller. For the first time in years, I was content—or as close to it as I could get. I made new friends, spent afternoons sharing tea and conversation with neighbors, and watched my daughter grow into a little person who truly delighted me.

Then I went on my first women's retreat, and in a moment of emotion, nothing would ever be the same again.

chapter eight

Laying Foundations

September 2002
Elkhart Lake, Wisconsin

The retreat, organized by Green Bay Community Church, was at Elkhart Lake, about two and a half hours from Green Bay. It was a spa-like retreat for women, with excellent music and equally awesome speakers.

After listening to a particularly inspiring message, we were divided into small groups where we were encouraged to share a few thoughts about our lives. When it came around to me, I was all prepared to talk about Daniel and the church and my daughter, but when I opened my mouth, I found myself talking instead about the sexual abuse I'd suffered at the hands of my stepfather.

Horrified, I began to cry. I tried to control it, but I was soon sobbing as if my heart would break. No one attempted to shut me up, and no one left the group in shock. Instead, they listened, and then one of the women took me back to the prayer room where she and another woman prayed with me.

It was such a cleansing weekend for me, and I actually felt lighter, as if a burden had been lifted. For years I'd tried to stay strong and ignore all the pain inside. When I had talked to Daniel about it, he told me that I couldn't live in the past, that I needed to move on, so that's what I had done. I covered it up and buried it as deep as I could—until the retreat, when it exploded. For the first time in my life, I felt such love and safety and protection that the old pain came pouring out like a fountain. It was as though an old festering wound in my heart had been opened, cleansed, and healed by God's love through the people who so kindly represented him. By the time I got home from the retreat, I was starting to feel as though I could handle anything.

Mom had moved to Arizona to be close to my sister Nadine, so I didn't hear from her often. But one day she called and invited us to fly down to Arizona for a few days. "Your sister is going to be out of town all week, and I'm watching my grandson, so why don't you all fly down and spend some time with me?"

I checked with Daniel and he agreed it would be a nice little getaway for us.

But Mom had a little surprise waiting for us when we arrived. My sister was not out of town after all, and in fact was more than a little annoyed that Mom had invited us. Nadine had never felt comfortable around Daniel. After deciding to keep her baby, she and the baby's father had gotten engaged, but the wedding never took place. Because she never married, she felt as though Daniel and his parents judged her.

Mom may have been hoping that throwing us all together in the same house would resolve old grudges, but it was not to be. In spite of the tension, however, we decided to enjoy ourselves. Daniel and I went to Mexico for a day, shopped, played golf, and hung out at the pool with the kids.

When we returned home, I dove headfirst into church activities at Green Bay Community Church—women's ministries, children's ministries, vacation Bible school, the Thrive conference (a leadership conference for women), one-on-one discipleship courses, and various Bible studies. I loved not working, and I loved hanging out with the women and children and sharing stories, child-rearing tips, and recipes. I enjoyed being able to decorate for every holiday, to spend time cooking, and to get to know my neighbors. I had turned from a career-driven woman into the Good Housekeeping church lady. Perhaps the role change seemed sudden, dramatic, and odd, but I felt like I'd finally come home.

To a lost little girl who never had a safe home or a place to belong, my church was like a dream come true. There I realized we have a wonderful, good Father who loves us. The church was a place where "brothers and sisters" could laugh and play and work and pray together. It was the home I'd never had. It was the haven my broken heart needed. Things were so good, Daniel and I decided it was time to start thinking about having another baby.

September 2003
Green Bay, Wisconsin

I had just been chosen to be a group leader in MOPS. I loved ministering to women—caring for others, doing for others, helping them with whatever problems they were going through at the time. It brought me a sense of fulfillment and peace I'd never experienced before. I realized that being needed in healthy ways was lovely.

I was on my way to one of those meetings one morning when I saw a woman coming up the street. She walked by our house every day with her dog—a beautiful Dalmatian that reminded Daniel of his childhood pet. As she came by, she greeted me with a wide smile and stopped to chat for a few minutes. "My name is Robin. My husband and I moved in down the street a couple months ago," she was telling me as I petted her dog. "We just love this neighborhood. Have you lived here long?"

"About five years. There are a lot of terrific ladies around the neighborhood. I'll have to introduce you to some of them."

"That would be wonderful." She tilted her head, studying me for a moment. "Don't I know you from somewhere?"

I shrugged. She did look vaguely familiar, but I couldn't place her. "I don't think so," I said.

"No. I'm sure we've met. Or I've seen you somewhere before. Where do you go to church?"

"St. Mark's. I used to be at Green Bay Community, but . . ."

But Daniel had put so much pressure on me that I finally spoke to one of the elders at the church, and he convinced me that maybe Daniel and I could find a church we both agreed on. We visited some churches and finally settled at St. Mark's. I still wasn't completely happy with the change, but I wanted to try for Daniel's sake.

Robin suddenly started laughing, apparently delighted. "You were at the retreat they sponsored last year, down in Elkhart Lake."

Suddenly it came to me. This was the lady at the retreat who had taken me to the prayer room and prayed for me. "Yes! You were so nice to me."

"You broke my heart." She reached over and gave me a hug. "Listen, I'm leading a Bible study at Green Bay Community Church. We're working on the book of John. Why don't you join us?"

"Sure. I'd love to."

"I just know we were supposed to meet again. I've prayed for you so often since the retreat."

Her words touched my heart. To think that someone I'd met only once had thought of me so often—and prayed for me. Maybe it was ordained for us to meet like this. And to become friends.

October 2003
Disney World, Orlando, Florida

We had not yet taken the trip to Disney World I had won, so Daniel and I finally packed our bathing suits, flip-flops, shorts, suntan lotion, and one very excited Sarah, and headed for Florida.

Sarah, now five years old, was a vivacious, bright, and outgoing charmer with long blond hair and an infectious smile. She made friends wherever she went and was determined to make Mickey, Goofy, and the Little Mermaid her new best friends. She chattered incessantly the entire flight, squirming impatiently to get there, see it all, and experience everything.

I too was mesmerized by Disney World—the different theme parks, the restaurants, the rides, the color, the characters, the parades, the fireworks, and the magic of it all.

Our first night there we sat in a restaurant and stared out at Cinderella's castle, all lit up for the evening.

"Daddy, are we going to see Mickey Mouse tomorrow?" Sarah gazed around, her mouth dappled by ketchup, her eyes lit up like fireflies. She was as captivated by the magic of the place as I was.

"Absolutely," Daniel assured her, wiping her mouth. "And we'll see Winnie the Pooh and Goofy and Cinderella."

"And the Little Mermaid?"

"And the Little Mermaid," he confirmed.

She let out a little sigh as she stared out at the castle. "I think I want to live here," she said.

I laughed but couldn't help half agreeing with her. Here there was nothing but fun. I looked at Daniel and marveled at the way he was always so solid, so sturdy—and immovable. But the very things that attracted me to him could also be a source of aggravation sometimes. He loved me and tended to be a little too protective, making me feel as though he were controlling me. But Dan was steady in the midst of turmoil—someone you could depend on no matter what. Above all, he loved being a husband and a father.

He was about to become a father again. I'd just found out I was pregnant and due in April. This trip was not only a gift to Sarah, it was a bit of a celebration for all of us. Once the baby was born, it would be a long time before we'd be able to travel like this again.

November 13, 2003
Green Bay, Wisconsin

I sat at the table trying to compose my thoughts and feelings. Mom had come back from Arizona to see us and was staying at her house up in Shawano, but we rarely got together. She would make plans to come and visit, but as had been her pattern in the past, she would cancel at the last minute or just not show up.

It was one thing for me to be disappointed, but when Sarah cried because her nana didn't come when she said she would, I knew I couldn't let it go on. I had to start protecting my daughter. Taking a deep breath, I put my pen to paper.

I told your granddaughter on Tuesday evening that you were in town and coming to visit on Friday and that you were going to have lunch with her at her kindergarten. She was so excited, she was jumping up and down in the kitchen. Sarah will be crushed when I have to tell her that her nana will not be coming now because she has to stay home and watch stocks on TV for her boyfriend.

Mom, it's been like this for ten years. I lived through seven years with one man always coming first in your life. Well, I'm still here. Where is he? And now it's another man. I've been a doormat to you. Most of the time you never show up or even call to say your plans have changed while I sit here waiting for you. Daniel asked me once why I put up with this behavior. I put up with it because I love you. But now I'm at my wit's end.

I am hurt and disappointed that you treat your daughter this way. And now it's starting to hurt my daughter. Sarah thinks the world of you, but I will not stand by and watch you set a day aside to see us and then cancel only to have her crushed.

If you would like to see me, you need to promise me that you will treat me with integrity, plan a day and time, and keep those plans—not cancel, or worse, not show up at all. I doubt if you treat the men in your life this way. If you cannot treat me with respect and make that promise to me, then I will not be able to see you until you can make and keep that promise.

If you can make that promise, then give me a call. If you can't, then maybe it would be a good idea to wait until you can.

With tears streaming down my face, I signed the letter, folded it, and put it in an envelope.

December 27, 2003
Green Bay, Wisconsin

The holidays were over, Mom hadn't spoken to me since receiving my letter, my pregnancy caused constant pain in my back, and I was sinking deep into a depression unlike any I'd suffered before.

Nothing seemed to help, not even soaking in the hot tub every night, but I kept up with the routine anyway.

One day in December, as I stepped onto the deck to turn on the jets in the tub, my feet hit ice and I was airborne. I slammed down on the deck, screaming as pain shot up my left side. The pain wrenched its way up my leg, into my hip and stomach, and then back down again. Ever so slowly I inched my way back inside the house to lie down. The next morning there was a bubble of skin sticking out of the groin area of my left thigh.

The doctor thought it was a hernia and wanted to operate right away, but my ob-gyn wouldn't give permission until after the baby was born. I was going to have to live with the excruciating pain for four more months.

By January I'd given up the MOPS leadership position and cut back on all my activities. I was still leading the one-on-one discipleship course, but it was pure determination that kept me going. I had to make sure the girls taking the course graduated. When I wasn't leading the course, I moved only from the bed to the recliner.

I was essentially bedridden. Unable to cook, clean, or care for Sarah, I placed a call, in sheer desperation, to my mother and asked her to come and help out. I was actually nervous about calling her, but the minute she gave me her answer, all nervousness fled.

"There's no way I can come up there, Tina. I have to watch the stocks."

"For the man I'm dating," she could have added (but didn't). It was always something for the man she was dating. My heart sank as I hung up the phone. I don't know why I was disappointed or even surprised. I cried bitterly for all that I would never have with my mom—the closeness, love, and respect.

Each day sent me further into a shroud of depression. The darkness seemed to pull me deeper and deeper into this black hole of suffocating pain and emotional emptiness. Doctors increased my meds, but nothing helped.

When the women at MOPS found out how bad things were at my house, they rallied together and came up with a plan. Some took turns cooking for my family, while others rotated the cleaning and laundry chores. They shopped, dusted, washed, vacuumed, and watched over Sarah.

They were so kind and giving, but in my depressed state, most days I barely noticed their presence. I slept or stared at the walls, barely conscious of anything going on around me. There were whispers of conversations, but I ignored them. The last months of the pregnancy became an oppressive blur of pain and emotional agony.

April 7, 2004
Green Bay, Wisconsin

I was so far beyond fatigue that I may have invented a whole new level of exhaustion. Labor had been endless, and the doctors couldn't seem to get my baby delivered. The baby was in distress, and I felt as if I were floating into oblivion—anything to try to escape the agony. Later the doctors would say I had "ripped from stem to stern." All I knew was that if they didn't get that baby out of me soon, I wasn't going to make it.

Suddenly the doctor called for a crash cart, and my thoughts started racing. They needed a defibrillator for me? No. My heart was still beating. That meant it was for my baby. Before I could speak, Daniel took my hand and comforted me. "It's okay, Tina. He'll be okay."

He. We had a little boy. Noah.

Noah was in pretty bad shape. He was born bruised and weak. The medical staff immediately put him on oxygen and whisked him off to ICU. I wanted to hold him, to cuddle him, but they had taken him away.

I stayed in the hospital for a week and was rarely able to see Noah. The highlight of my day came when they would take me down to ICU, get him out of the special unit they had him in, and place him in my arms. Afterward the nurse would take me down to sit in the whirlpool. It was the only thing that gave me any relief from the pain.

After a week, I was sent home—without my baby. Daniel took care of everything with the help of my friends from MOPS. Between the back pain, the injury from the fall, the pain from the delivery, all the stitches, and the emotional pain from the depression, I was barely aware of my own existence. The fact that I'd given birth to a child was somehow lost to me as I spiraled deeper and deeper into this abyss of emotional and physical pain.

A few days after coming home from the hospital, I was cleared to have the surgery that I needed after the fall on the ice. I was so ready for some relief. After the surgery, the doctor came in to talk to me. "It was a mess in there, Tina. It was a mess. We had to reconstruct the blood vessels. They were about to burst. However, I think we repaired them all."

Even though the blood vessels had been fixed, there was still the lingering pain that followed the surgery. My life had turned into one big mountain of pain. It was hard to distinguish which hurt more, my body or my spirit. I just couldn't handle it anymore and slowly gave up trying to fight, slipping further and further into that dark shroud from which there was no escape.

I have very little memory of those days, weeks, or months. Most of what I know has come from family and friends telling me how bad I was—that I showed no interest in Noah and, in fact, gave no indication that I even realized he was my baby. I slept or stared at the walls. I didn't speak; I didn't respond; I didn't seem to be aware of anything or anyone.

April slipped into May. During the day Daniel's mother came over to take care of Noah and me. Daniel worked all day at the office, then came home to feed the children, give them their baths, and put them to bed. He had to get up several times during the night to care for Noah.

By the end of May, Daniel knew something more had to be done. He called my mother and begged her to come help us out. "Tina is in so much pain, she can't care for the children or the house. I have to work and get up at night to feed Noah and get Sarah off to school and cook and clean. My parents have been helping out, but they're exhausted too. Please come help us. Tina needs you."

She surprised everyone by agreeing to come. However, I was oblivious to her presence.

For a week, my mother took over running the house and taking care of Sarah and Noah while I remained emotionally and mentally withdrawn from everything around me. A couple of times Mom managed to get me up and dressed and out for a walk around the neighborhood. But these excursions were tiny little slivers of light that never lasted. When she left, I cried, enveloped again by the dark cloud around me.

June 9, 2004
Bellin Psychiatric Health Clinic

Daniel, having run out of options to help me, finally took me to Bellin Psychiatric Clinic for help. The doctor talked with me for more than an hour, asking me about my pregnancy, my child's birth, and even my past.

I had lost twenty-seven pounds since Noah's birth. Most women would celebrate that, but my weight loss occurred because of nausea, vomiting, and diarrhea—not exactly a pleasant diet plan.

The doctor diagnosed major depressive disorder, "recurrent and severe, without psychosis, of a postpartum nature." In addition, he told me I had "a panic disorder with agoraphobia."

I stumbled on that last word. "What do you mean, 'agoraphobia'? What's that?"

He propped his elbows on his desk and folded his hands. "It's a condition where a patient has a fear of having anxiety attacks, losing control, or embarrassing themselves in situations to such an extent that they remain in a painful state of anxious anticipation because of those fears. You become restricted or housebound to hide."

Hiding felt familiar. I'd been hiding my whole life. Starting out, I'd hid behind smiles and perfect behavior, then I hid behind compliance, then behind submission, and now I hid under covers and behind closed doors.

I was in Bellin for a week and then released. But I didn't really feel any better—just well medicated.

June 28, 2004
Green Bay, Wisconsin

I stood in the kitchen for over an hour, staring blindly at the refrigerator. I was supposed to be making dinner, but I couldn't focus enough to decide what to make, much less how to make it. Picking up the phone, I called Darla, one of my friends from MOPS, and asked if she could possibly bring a meal over.

When Darla arrived she had Cassie, another MOPS friend, with her. While Cassie sat down in the living room with me and tried to engage me in conversation, Darla went downstairs.

When she returned, she said to Cassie, "The freezer is packed with dinners."

"Then why did she call us?" Cassie asked.

Darla pulled out a chair next to me. "Look at her, Cassie. I don't think she knows what she's doing."

I looked up at them and said, "I'm thinking of getting Noah and going over to the Tower Drive Bridge."

"Why would you want to do that, Tina?" Cassie asked.

I didn't know. While I searched through my scattered thoughts for the answer, I heard myself say, "To jump off."

chapter nine

Sinking in the Mire

June 28, 2004
Green Bay, Wisconsin

Horrified, Cassie and Darla looked at each other, trying to figure out if I was serious. My mind faded out of the reality at hand, and I lost interest in the conversation. The phone rang, but I didn't care who was calling or why. I turned and stared out the patio doors while Cassie answered the phone.

I heard her mention my name and tell someone that I was acting strangely. Normally I would have been offended by that. At this point, however, I couldn't have reacted if I had wanted to. It seemed to take twenty minutes for my brain to register what it was hearing, and by the time I understood what someone had said, it was too late to bother responding. I was in a thick fog of confusion, saying things that surprised me while unable to put into words what I wanted to say.

When Daniel came home from work, a flurry of conversation started up between my friends and my husband. They were talking about me as if I couldn't hear them, and on some level I really couldn't. I would hear the words, but I couldn't understand what anyone was actually saying.

"She's in bad shape, Daniel. Look at her. She's like a zombie. You talk to her and it takes her forever to form an answer. Her speech is slurred. Her eyes aren't focused. You need to get her help, and you need to get it for her now."

Daniel glanced over at me. "Well, I know she's been depressed. The doctor said that she has postpartum depression again."

"She's worse, Daniel. The medications aren't helping her. We've already called her friend Rachael, and she's coming over to watch the kids. Let's get Tina to the hospital."

Daniel paused for a moment, then said, "I need to call her brother first. He needs to know what's going on."

At that point, one of my friends picked up the phone and handed it to him. "Call him."

Daniel took the phone and left the room. Rachael arrived to take care of the children, and within minutes I was whisked out the door and off to the hospital.

I put up some resistance, but it wasn't enough to get anyone to take me seriously. Some part of me didn't want to go to the hospital, but I lacked the wherewithal to dig my heels in and refuse.

When we arrived at Bellin Psychiatric Health Center, there were so many people around and it all seemed so loud and chaotic that my apprehension at being there greatly increased. Cassie came in with Daniel and me. When we sat down in front of the admissions clerk, I knew that I had to let them know I didn't need to be there. I struggled to answer the questions put to me, using every ounce of concentration to stay focused on the clerk.

"Are you suicidal?" she asked me, pen poised over the paper she was filling out.

"No," I insisted.

Immediately Cassie jumped in. "Earlier today she was muttering about taking the baby and jumping off the Tower Drive Bridge."

Daniel looked shocked as he turned to face me. "Teen, is that true?"

"Yes," I found myself responding.

Then I kept saying, "I don't belong here; I don't belong here." But they were no longer listening to me. I was admitted, taken to my room, and monitored for the next four days while they tried to get my depression under control with medications and therapy.

Nine of my girlfriends formed a prayer group while I was in the hospital. They made a commitment to meet once a week at Robin's house, and for hours they prayed for my recovery and for my family. They would, in my opinion, become the linchpin of my recovery. Nine women took time away from their own lives to come together and pray for me—not because they had to, not because someone asked them to, but simply because they cared enough to make a commitment to seek the Lord's help, and they stuck to it.

I was discharged from the hospital on July 1 with a bag of medications from the doctor and countless well wishes from the staff. After I got home, Cassie came by to see how I was doing. I took her by the hand and led her into my bedroom, where I pointed to the medicine bottles lined up like an infantry ready for an invasion.

"See all this?" I asked her. "All this, but I don't feel any better. You think they're going to help you, but you take all these drugs, and they don't make you feel better. They only make you feel nothing."

A few days later, I reached my limit. I couldn't stand the pain, the depression, the confusion, the fatigue, the medications, the loss of appetite, and the sleeplessness. Daniel was in the kitchen making dinner and I was helping him when I suddenly just exploded, flailing around the kitchen and scaring Daniel.

He calmed me down and put me to bed. "I'm calling your mother, Teen. We need her help."

I didn't care if he called her or not. I just rolled over and closed my eyes, shutting everything out. I wanted only one thing: an end to the relentless pain. I was getting to the point of ultimate desperation, the point where I would do anything to make it all stop.

Kyle stopped by the next day, and Daniel told him that Mom was flying up from Arizona. Pulling out a kitchen chair, my brother sat down. He glanced briefly in my direction before turning his attention back to Daniel. "What is she doing coming back here again? She just left."

"Tina is having a hard time, Kyle. I thought it best that your mom come up and try to get her back in shape."

"Daniel, you know how our mom is. She thinks the answer to everything is tough love, and Tina doesn't respond to that kind of thing."

My husband dropped down in a chair, propping his elbows on the table and running his fingers through his hair. "I don't know what else to try, Kyle. I'm running out of options."

"Well," Kyle conceded, compassion for Daniel overtaking his common sense, "you never know. It might work."

July 8, 2004
Shawano, Wisconsin

When my mom arrived, she took me back to Shawano to stay at her home. I was nearly catatonic at this point, barely able to respond to questions and taking forever to answer the simplest inquiry. My mother would get me up and make me get dressed, then take me out for long walks, visits with neighbors and old friends, or picnics at the lake. I went along without resistance, like a compliant child being led by the hand.

The only thing I cared about or thought about was food. I was hungry all the time, which was very unlike me. I was always wondering when the next meal was coming, even while finishing the one in front of me.

I never thought about my husband and children. I wasn't even aware that I had a family unless they were right in front of me.

While I was staying with my mother, she and Daniel were working with my doctor to get me started on electroconvulsive therapy (ECT), but the insurance company was slow in approving the treatment. Every day there was a flurry of phone calls between Daniel, my mom, and the doctor, and every day it was the same frustrating answer: "Not yet."

While my family battled with the insurance company, trying to get help for me, I was sinking further into utter despair. I thought more and more about preferring death to the endless pain. I'd heard of people whose mind snapped when pain became unbearable. Wasn't this, after all, the point of physical torture? It was used to wear down all emotional defenses until nothing mattered but stopping the pain. I understood how people in terrible, endless, chronic pain felt. Unending pain, emotional or physical, turns the normal world into a terrifying fight for survival. Long-term sleep deprivation can make the sanest soul crazy. Not only did I suffer from the stitches that were needed after the delivery, but the pain from the surgery and the back injury kept me from sleeping in spite of the pills I was taking. I'd doze for a couple of hours and then get up and walk around, sometimes unaware that I was even doing it. Once my mother found me pacing in the hall about three in the morning.

"What are you doing up?" she mumbled, brushing her hair back off her face.

"I couldn't sleep."

"Well, just go back to bed!" She turned on her heel, went back into her room, and shut the door firmly behind her.

The next day we drove up to Michigan for a family reunion. As we traveled, I stared out the window, oblivious to the beauty of a brilliant summer day. Mom had tried to pull me into a conversation a couple of times, but I couldn't focus on the words, so I didn't bother trying to find answers or comments.

The only thing I remember about the reunion was seeing Sarah. Daniel had brought her, but she would barely look at me. She was so sad, and maybe a bit angry at not being able to be with me every day.

Back in Shawano on a Friday night, some of my friends came by to take me to a church for a healing service. They were determined that I was going to go and that I would be healed. However, the place terrified me. As my friends tried to walk me up to the altar for prayer, I was backpedaling right out the door. They realized that the miracle they'd longed for wasn't going to happen that night. Sadly they drove me back home.

On Saturday Daniel came and took me out boating with a friend of his, hoping that being out on the lake would help me feel better. I sat near the stern and stared out across the water, wishing I could contribute something to the conversation. But there were two obstacles I couldn't overcome: I had nothing to say and even if I did, words wouldn't form. If you've ever been underwater and looked up, only vaguely aware of sound and shadow above you, then you have some idea of what I felt like—all the time.

The day was breathtakingly beautiful, the lake like glass, but it didn't impress me any more than sitting on my bed, staring at the walls did.

I needed to end the pain somehow. I just wasn't sure how to accomplish it. The medications weren't helping. If anything, they seemed to make things worse. I couldn't form thoughts, couldn't get my brain cells to function through the heavy blanket of medication to create opinions or speech. I was just a lifeless "thing"—breathing but worthless. I knew everyone would be better off if I were dead. It would end my misery and relieve their burden.

The more I thought about it, the more sense it made to end my life. A person could endure only so much pain and misery, and there was a limit to what everyone around me could take as well. Daniel was working without a break, stressed from being at his job all day and then hurrying home to take care of our children. Noah woke him several times during the night, so Daniel was getting very little sleep. My mother was totally frustrated trying to cope with me. My friends were constantly praying for me.

I needed to give them all the freedom to move on with their own lives. There was no longer any hope for me.

chapter ten

The Jump off
Tower Drive Bridge

July 19, 2004

It was another bright sunny day. Mom made plans for us to put together a picnic lunch and head to Shawano Lake for the day. I stood in the kitchen, leaning against the counter while she moved from cupboard to cabinet, gathering the food she planned to take with us.

My daughter, Sarah, visiting me for the day, was sitting in the living room, watching cartoons.

As I stood watching my mother, she turned quickly to face me. "Why can't you just get over this depression?" she shot at me.

"Don't you think I would if I could?"

"Then snap out of it!" she continued. "You're like a zombie most of the time. And the rest of the time, you're asleep."

I leaned back against the counter, her words wounding me like a knife to the heart.

I glanced down and saw my car keys just inches from my hand, and suddenly I knew what I had to do. Grabbing the keys, I ran out the door. I could hear my mother screaming behind me, but I ignored her, climbed into the car, and locked the doors. Sarah came running out of the house behind my mother, who began pounding on the car window. I put the car in reverse and hit the gas.

Gravel spit as I peeled off down the driveway, nearly knocking my mother over in the process. Putting the car into drive, I raced up the street and around the corner. I had to make it to the bridge. If I could make it to the bridge, the pain would stop. I just had to make it to the bridge, and the hopelessness would end.

It became a refrain, running over and over in my head as I raced down the highway: *make it to the bridge, and the pain will end.*

It's hopeless. Just wanna die. Make it to the bridge.

As I sped down the highway, I saw Daniel's Durango coming up the highway toward me. My mom must have called him. I watched in the rearview mirror after I passed him. He cut through the median, making a U-turn, and started to follow me. I couldn't let him stop me.

I floored it, hitting over a hundred miles an hour, determined to make it to the bridge.

The next time I looked in the rearview mirror, I saw a police car behind me, lights flashing.

I had to get to the bridge. I couldn't let him stop me. I looked down at my speedometer—a hundred and twenty miles an hour.

I had to make it.

Daniel had called the police the moment he saw my car on the highway. State Police Officer Les Boldt had just gone off duty and had stopped by the post office to mail in his time card. He had been told to keep to the back roads on his way home so he wouldn't have to respond to a call. A call would mean paperwork, and paperwork would mean overtime.

After dropping his time card in the mailbox, he returned to his car and heard the call come over the radio. "A woman is racing down the highway and heading for the Tower Drive Bridge." Ignoring his orders, Officer Boldt flipped on his lights and quickly made his way down Packerland to Highway 41.

I drove past him just as he reached the intersection.

He pulled out onto the highway right behind me, keeping pace with my car. As I came off the exit to Highway 43, I passed another police car coming down 43. Sergeant Bill Morgan pulled out behind Officer Boldt.

I ignored them as I took the exit for the bridge. All my thoughts were focused on that bridge. I had to make it to the bridge. If I could just make it to the bridge, the pain would stop.

When I finally reached the highest point of Tower Drive

Video stills from police dash camera.

Bridge, I pulled over and stopped the car. I was so calm, so sure. I knew this was the right thing to do, and I felt peace as I opened the door, stepped out, and walked around my car toward the guardrail.

The Tower Drive Bridge had recently been renamed the Leo Frigo Bridge, but most lifelong residents of Green Bay rarely used the new name. It was the highest bridge in the state of Wisconsin, rising some two hundred feet above the Fox River. I knew it was the perfect spot. Two others had recently jumped off this bridge and neither survived.

As I reached the concrete barrier, I heard someone calling out to me.

"Ma'am! Ma'am!"

I ignored him as I took a deep breath . . . and jumped . . . headfirst over the barrier toward the river below.

State Police Officer Les Boldt was no rookie. He knew that

he was supposed to come up along the driver's side of my car and circle around the front of it to approach me. He had also been well trained in dealing with a "jumper." The policy dictated that the officer should never risk his own life to stop the one jumping.

He ignored both procedures as he pulled his cruiser up behind me (dash cam rolling) and then ran in front of his car to the passenger's side of mine—the shortest route to me. In miraculous, split-second timing, Officer Boldt reached out and snagged my wrist just as I went down over the edge.

My body weight nearly dragged him over with me, and if it hadn't been for a narrow ledge that I hit as I went over, breaking my momentum, we both would have fallen into the river. He bent his knees, locking them against the concrete wall as he held on. I tried to fight him off, begging him to let me go.

"I have you. I'm not letting you go," he said firmly.

His words irritated me. I wanted to go. I wanted to plunge down and die. I wanted the pain to stop. I wanted the misery to end. I just wanted to die.

But he wouldn't let me go.

I grabbed a cable and tried to pull loose from his grip, to no avail.

And then suddenly there were two other officers there, helping him pull me back over the barrier.

Deputy Kevin Kinard grabbed my legs and set me down. "On the ground. Down on the ground," he instructed.

As they set me down on the road, one of them knelt down and asked, "What hospital would you like to go to?"

The first thing I thought of was the kind ladies who had taken care of me when I had given birth to Noah. "Aurora," I answered.

A police officer had stopped Daniel about a mile from the bridge. This was standard procedure. If I succeeded in jumping, they didn't want Daniel to see it. But they couldn't stop him from seeing it play out in his mind as he sat in the police car and answered questions.

As if his fears weren't bad enough, he heard Sergeant Morgan's transmission crackling over the police radio: "She jumped!"

His heart broke as he struggled to comprehend it. Shaking, he sat in that patrol car and fought back tears.

But then he heard another transmission. "Four-Ida, we have the woman. Requesting medical assistance."

"Ten-four, Ida. Requesting medical."

Daniel pulled out his cell phone and called my mother, breaking down on the phone as he let her know I was safe and on my way to the hospital.

When Daniel arrived at the hospital, he found me handcuffed to the bed.

"Why, Tina? Why would you do this?"

I didn't bother answering as I mourned the fact that I had failed.

Sergeant Morgan stepped into my room and signaled to Daniel, leading him out into the hall. "Mr. Zahn, I just need to tell you that the press has gotten ahold of the story. It's going to be all over the news tonight."

"Oh, no. Just what we need."

Morgan put a hand on Daniel's shoulder. "I'm doing all I can to keep your names out of it."

"Thank you. I appreciate that."

"You know, Mr. Zahn, I've been at this job a long time and I can tell you that you are one lucky man. Everything had to be perfect from the time you called in. If just one piece had been out of place, the outcome would have been very different."

Daniel just stared at him as every conceivable emotion seemed to roll, one on top of the other, within him.

"If you hadn't seen her. If Officer Boldt had obeyed orders and gone home. If I hadn't been parked near that intersection. If I hadn't had five officers working on this side of the river today." Bill Morgan took a deep breath, nearly as caught up in the emotion of the events as my husband was. "Someone was looking out for your wife today. Someone was praying."

How right he was. Nine women to be exact.

My brother, Kyle, was sitting in his home office when he received a call from our cousin who worked for the Brown County Sheriff's Department. "Kyle? Your sister tried to jump off the bridge."

Thinking it was a joke, Kyle replied, "How do you know this and I don't?"

"One of the officers called me, knowing I was related to Tina."

As our cousin related the events, Kyle realized she was serious. He hung up the phone and raced upstairs, calling his wife, "Sarah! Sarah!"

Sarah, in the baby's room, stuck her head out the door. "What?"

"It's Tina. She tried to jump off the bridge." He spun around in a circle. "What am I gonna do?"

Sarah reached out to him. "Calm down. She's fine, right?"

It took a minute for Kyle to respond as his thoughts raced as fast as his heart. "Yes, but she could have died today. A cop caught her. Dear God, she was almost gone, and he caught her."

"Okay, calm down."

"I need to go to the hospital. Where are my keys?" Kyle started searching through his pockets. "I don't know where my keys are."

Sarah glanced back in the nursery, making sure that the baby had slept through Kyle's panic before easing the door closed. "I'll find your keys, just take a deep breath. It'll be okay."

Back at Aurora Hospital, Daniel was rushing between doctors, nurses, and the police, as well as taking calls from all our friends who saw the news report and making phone calls to his parents to keep them apprised of the latest developments. Making his life more difficult, my mom had arrived. In her own state of shock, she was running around, giving the medical staff orders and making demands that only added to the confusion.

Daniel was existing on his last drop of energy as he signed the papers for me to be transferred over to Bellin Clinic.

When Kyle showed up, panicked and shaking, he found Daniel at the nurse's station. "How is she?"

Daniel looked up, surprised to see my brother. "How did you find out?"

"My cousin called me. How is she?"

"She's fine. Out of it, but okay."

Kyle took a deep breath and leaned against the counter. "I saw the police video on the news just as I was leaving the house. I can't believe she did this. I mean, I saw her do it on television, but it's so hard to get that into my brain, you know?"

"I know. Listen, why don't you go in and see her for a minute. They're getting ready to transfer her over to Bellin, and then I need you to do me a favor."

"Anything. Name it."

"Go get my dad, and the two of you see about getting Teen's car out of compound. Her purse is still in it and I think we're going to need some of Teen's identification. There's a Sergeant Bill Morgan downstairs. He can tell you the specifics."

Kyle nodded. "I'll take care of it."

As soon as I was registered at Bellin, I was placed in what they call the "Cranberry Unit." I was dressed in a kind of jumpsuit that high-risk patients have to wear to minimize any risk of self-injury.

What struck me first was how dark it felt in there. It was cold, dark, and very stark—a few chairs and a table. There was one other person in the unit—a woman who, like me, had tried to injure herself.

Aside from my family, two of my first visitors were my pastor from Green Bay Community Church and the pastor from St. Mark's Lutheran Church, who gave me his Bible to use. Daniel quickly brought my Bible to the hospital for me and returned the pastor's Bible, but I had no interest in reading it.

There was a steady stream of visitors day after day—my

MOPS friends, ladies from the church, neighbors, and of course family members, but I barely acknowledged their presence as I sat staring into space.

Daniel sat in the living room with his parents and tried to give them an update on my condition, but each time he opened his mouth, the phone would ring.

"Hello?" Daniel would listen for a few seconds, then put his hand over the receiver to speak to his family. "Another reporter."

As soon as he could get a word in, he would say, "No comment," and hang up the phone.

"How many does that make today?" Kyle asked at one point.

"I lost count at ten. And it's more than just reporters now. It's also the talk shows."

Greatgram's eyes went wide. "Are you serious?"

"You know what is really sad about all this?" Kyle interjected. "No one cared when she was sinking further and further into this depression. They only care when she did something so drastic she almost lost her life. Now they want to know how she feels. Where was all this attention when she really needed it?"

"I'll tell you what's worse." Dan reached over and picked up his can of Coke. "Today the doctor told me that postpartum depression is always worse with each successive pregnancy. I was furious. Why didn't they warn us it could be worse?"

"Would you have had Noah if you'd known?" my sister-in-law asked.

"Yes," Dan said, "but at least we would have known what to

look for and we would have been prepared for it, rather than scrambling around trying to figure out what it was and not getting any answers until it was too late."

I was finally moved out of the Cranberry Unit and into a private room. Then I had my own bathroom and shower, but the room was as dark and dismal as the unit I left.

As soon as the insurance company found out about my jump, they immediately approved all the ECT treatments the doctor had prescribed for me. The first time I had the treatment, I felt like a whole new person—for about forty-five minutes—before slowly sinking back down into hopelessness again. The effects of the second treatment lasted about two hours. The third had me feeling better for almost the whole day. Little by little, I was pulled out of my dark despair.

The only problem was that each time I went in for the ECT, I would forget everything that happened prior to going in for the treatment. Daniel would laugh and call it "Groundhog Day," because each time I would come out saying, "Why am I here? What day is it?"

My favorite time of day was making crafts in occupational therapy. I had always loved anything to do with art, and some of my favorite times with Sarah were sitting at the kitchen table making macaroni jewelry or painting pictures with her.

I went through my days at Bellin in innocent oblivion, caught up in the routine of treatments, therapy, and sleep, unaware of the chaos I'd left in my wake.

While I was making pottery (and some progress emotionally),

Daniel, his family, my mom, my brother, and my sister-in-law had meetings to discuss the big question—what next? There were meetings with the doctors, treatments to be discussed, meals to be prepared, children to be cared for, a house to be kept clean and running, jobs to do, and visits to the hospital.

Deborah and Greatgram volunteered to take the children during the day. Daniel would drop the kids off at his mother's, go to work from eight to five, swing by the hospital to talk to the doctors and have dinner with me, go pick up the kids, take them home and put them to bed, sleep a little in between Noah's feedings, only to wake up and do it all over again the next day.

My mom didn't stay in town long after I was admitted to Bellin. She didn't like the doctor who was caring for me because she didn't feel he was particularly concerned with my best interests. Daniel didn't want to switch doctors, especially since the insurance company had finally approved the ECT treatments that were helping me. Mom insisted on firing the doctor and getting another one; Daniel refused. When the battle of wills reached a certain point, Daniel recommended my mom return home. She left for Arizona the next day.

As for me, I began to feel bored and restless. I wanted to go home.

August 6, 2004
Bellin Psychiatric Health Center
Green Bay, Wisconsin

I reread all my answers on the recovery form. I was going home, as long as I finished the form correctly, that is. The question I

Sergeant Bill Morgan (far left), Deputy Kevin Kinard (second from left), and Trooper Les Boldt (far right) at a ceremony honoring them for saving Tina's life.

was working on was, "What are ten things you can do to take care of yourself?" I had given all the pat answers I knew to give—exercise, eat healthy, get plenty of sleep, hobbies.

Smiling, I wrote my last answer: "Stay away from tall bridges." That should make them laugh.

Handing in the form, I went back to packing up my possessions. Daniel would be picking me up in a few minutes, and I couldn't wait to get home. Walking over to the window, I stared out across the parking lot.

I knew I wasn't cured. I had a long road of recovery ahead of me. We had the PPD under some control, but I had years of abuse, denial, and repressed anger to wade through.

All my life I'd tried to hide pain. As a child, I hid how much it hurt to be abused and rejected. As a teen, I hid how much it hurt to be repeatedly betrayed. As a young woman, I hid the pain of two abortions. As a woman, I hid the pain of back and arm injuries. I took medications to mask the pain and to keep on going, and I wore a mask to keep people from knowing the truth. But no matter how hard you try to outrun the past and the pain, it catches up with you. The harder you try to ignore it, the harder it will take you down.

Now I had to learn to face the past, forgive people, accept who I was, and learn to love myself. It wasn't going to be easy.

The road to healing would start with my realizing that I could either go on being a victim or I could choose to be a victor. I could go under or I could overcome.

I wanted to overcome.

chapter eleven

Groundhog Day

September 2004
Green Bay, Wisconsin

After I came home from the hospital, we came up with a
schedule for taking care of the children so that I could
ease back into life and not be overwhelmed. I got up in the
morning and got Sarah ready for school. Daniel would get Noah
fed and changed. Then he would drop Sarah off at school and
take Noah to his mom's house for the day. Daniel's mother
made meals and sent them home with Daniel and Noah a
couple times a week.

Once everyone was out the door, the silence would bring
tears to my eyes. My back pain was still so severe I couldn't
even pick up my baby. I missed him and wanted to mother
him, but my body would not allow me that privilege. I would

sit in the house all day alone and fight the depression. It's not that I didn't want to get back to normal. I desperately wanted to feel good again. The doctors told me that when someone has a clinical depression as severe as mine was, it's best to come back to normal life slowly. I didn't like hearing that. Patience has never been a virtue of mine—I wanted to get well right away.

The doctors urged me to focus on *me* for this period of time as the first step in getting better. So I signed up for MOPS again, hoping that getting back in sync with the other moms I'd so enjoyed at church would take my mind off missing Noah during the day. I also signed up for a women's ministry study called "Clothed in the Colors of His Love," but I couldn't get motivated to read my Bible or study. I had no interest at all.

Then, in week four of the study, I saw the words "get ready to be amazed," and they made such an impression on me that I circled them. Curious, I kept reading. It said that God brings beauty out of the ashes and that we should live in the light not in the dark. The words, one small phrase at a time, began to penetrate.

Little by little, my attention span lengthened, my interest came back, and I found myself enjoying the study of Scripture again. However, I was still on numerous medications that made me groggy in the morning. I had a hard time simply crawling out of bed. I'd have to ask God to help me with the most mundane things: "Lord, give me the strength to sit up. Now would you help me to stand and get dressed?" I know that people in depression must look lazy and selfish to others who are not, but take my word for it, sometimes it takes more courage for clinically depressed people to simply get up in the morning and put one foot in front of the other than it does for those whose brains are balanced to climb a mountain.

One of the brightest lights in those days was my neighbor and friend Robin. She had gone through a depression of her own years earlier and understood how hard it was to fight through to recovery. So almost every day she'd stop in, dropping off inspiring and cheerful cards, giving me hugs, encouraging me to start journaling, praying with me, and most of all, helping me understand that those who had suffered the most often had the most to offer others.

November 2004
Green Bay, Wisconsin

On November 6 I started seeing a counselor whom a close friend had recommended. After listening to my story, the first thing she did was have me join a twelve-step program at Green Bay Community Church. I especially needed to understand the first principle of the program: we are powerless and our lives are unmanageable without God.

It was a liberating moment to realize that all this "stuff" I was trying to carry wasn't mine to carry anymore. I could lay it all down and let it go. What had happened to me as a child wasn't because I was bad or ugly or unlovable. It happened because my stepfather had a problem he couldn't control and my mother didn't know how to deal with it.

To live in the light is to be truthful about how you feel, not to hide behind a mask of compliance or perfection or fear or hopelessness. It doesn't mean you gloss over the pain or abuse in your past, but it does mean that you get to choose whether or not you'll remain a victim. You can continue to let your abuser victimize you by sabotaging your current life, or you can stand up for yourself and refuse to be a victim anymore. I love the line from *My Big Fat Greek Wedding:* "Do not let the past dictate who you are, but let it become a part of who you will be."

The truth is, I had more than one problem assaulting me, making my case truly complicated. We could get the PPD under control, but there were still the issues from the past that had to be sorted out and dealt with, there was the back pain to push through, and there were the effects of so many medications. I was suffering from multiple traumas. Just like an accident victim with multiple injuries may need a whole team of doctors to tend to the various traumas, so it has taken (and still takes) a village of supportive people to help me in my recovery.

For the back pain, I began to wear a TENS unit. It sends electrical pulses to the muscle and interrupts the pain signal to the brain. I still wear this unit around the clock. The sticky pads that attach to my skin often cause open wounds that also have to be treated.

For the anxiety and depression I was taking a series of medications that left me groggy, fatigued, hungover, and headachy.

I wanted instant relief, but I had to realize that it wasn't going to happen that way.

The next thing my counselor had me work on was how

to create healthy boundaries. I had always allowed people to walk all over me, use me, or push me into doing things I didn't want to do. I started setting new boundaries with my mother-in-law. I loved Deborah—she's one of the sweetest ladies I've ever known—but I had allowed her to move into places in my life and marriage where she didn't belong. I didn't blame her; I realized that I hadn't been able to be the wife and mother to my family that they needed, and Deborah had to assume some of my roles during that time.

I was also a people pleaser who didn't want to upset anyone, so it was impossible for Deborah to know the feelings I had been unwilling to express. But the time had come to set boundaries and to begin to take more responsibility for myself and my family. After discussing my concerns and making some positive adjustments with Deborah, I moved on to my other relationships. I started setting healthy boundaries with Daniel and then with my friends. It wasn't always easy speaking up when I didn't agree with someone or telling people how I really felt.

It was also a time of growing up, letting go, and accepting the loss of dreams that could never be realized. One of those dreams was that my mother would find a way to bond with me in a loving mother-daughter relationship. I had a fantasy of the mother I wanted her to be that collided over and over again with the reality of who she was. She was never going to be the mother I longed for because, regardless of the circumstances, in her mind, I had been the object of her husband's attention. It didn't matter that I had never wanted it, had died a small death every time he touched me, and had wished she would notice and protect me. I had been with her husband sexually, and as far as she was concerned, we could never have the kind of mother-daughter relationship I wanted. I had to close the door on that fantasy, grieve its loss, and leave the crumpled dream in God's hands. I would never have the all-forgiving, understanding, and comforting mother I desired.

There were good days and bad days. Christmas was a hard day. We were with Daniel's family at their home, and it was everything Christmas should be—the tree, the gifts, the laughter, the food, the lights, the children. Daniel's brother, Michael, came in like a second Santa, making trip after trip from his little VW Bug, hauling in presents, most of them for Sarah.

Sarah had gone through a rough summer with my being in and out of the hospital with the depression, and with everyone focusing on my getting well. The poor child didn't even have a birthday party. Well, her uncle Mike was making up for that now, showering her with Christmas gifts and making the day truly special for her.

I watched Sarah and her uncle interact and marveled at the love this family had for one another. When I started to cry, Daniel came to me, got down on his knees, and asked, "Why are you crying?"

Michael looked over at me, his face suddenly drawn with concern.

"I miss my family," I told them. It was tearing me up that my family was scattered—and shattered. Of course, I had wanted my mom to get out of her dysfunctional marriage with my stepfather, but I had hoped that she and I would be closer once he was gone. Instead, I had always felt as though she had divorced me along with my stepfather.

The illusion my parents had presented to the world was of a close-knit, well-adjusted, loving family. For a child, an illusion is sometimes hard to differentiate from reality. I was still holding on to the illusion, but reality was smacking me in the face. Nadine and Matthew lived in Arizona, as did my mother. We rarely spoke to or saw each other. And when I did have interaction with my mother or Nadine, there was always tension.

My sister Whitney and I were a little bit closer, especially with her living in the Green Bay area, but it still wasn't the sisterly relationship I longed for.

On the other hand, there was Kyle. He was more brother than most girls could ever ask for. He was always there for me, always loving me, always supportive of my best interests.

It was hard letting go of the deep desire to be close to my family. I wanted to share holidays and birthdays and everyday events, to know that they cared enough to be there when I needed them, loved me without conditions, and needed me as much as I needed them.

Kneeling there on the floor, Daniel took my hand. "We're your family, Teen. We love you."

Sometimes our blood relatives are all the family we need; sometimes God sets the lonely in families made up of a variety of friends and nurturing souls.

December gave way to January, and I was going in for ECT once a month. On the days that I had the treatments, Daniel and I would have to get up at four in the morning. Deborah and Greatgram would come over to watch the kids.

The treatments were given at Bellin Psychiatric Health Center and were set up so that the first person to sign in was the first person to be treated. Daniel and I tried to get there as early as possible—usually about 5:20, so that I could get my treatment and get out as quickly as possible.

Once we arrived, Dan would go nap in the waiting room while I headed for the ECT unit. On the way I passed the children's unit, and it was horrible to think that these little children were suffering from depression severe enough to need ECT. What could have happened to these children in their short lives to bring them to this unit?

After I signed in, I was taken to a room and prepped for the treatment. An IV hookup was inserted on the top of my left hand for the anesthesiologist, and electrodes were placed on my temples.

About half an hour later, the anesthesiologist would come through to administer the medications that would put me to sleep and temporarily paralyze my muscles. The anesthesiologists were all business—cool, detached, professional. As if these treatments weren't scary enough, their detachment only made the experience worse. Thankfully there was Nurse Fitzgerald. She was a real sweetheart, going from patient to patient, offering a comforting word and a warm smile. She'd hold my right hand while the anesthesiologist hooked up the IV on my left.

"Okay." The anesthesiologist slowly injected a succinylcholine and barbiturate cocktail into the IV. "You're going to feel a slight burn."

Sure enough, by the time he placed the oxygen mask over my face, I could feel the warmth in my hand—spreading up my arm.

"You're going to feel a little drowsy."

Nurse Fitzgerald stroked my right hand. "It's okay, dear. You're doing just fine."

I was barely aware of the doctor, who at this point would begin hooking up the machine to the electrodes on my temples.

Half an hour later I would wake up wondering where I was and why I was there. The medical personnel would unhook me, get me dressed, and lead me back to Daniel.

"What am I doing here?" I always asked him.

He smiled, "Groundhog Day."

Each and every time, he'd walk me to the car and explain everything all over again. I'm not sure where he got the patience. But after each of the treatments, he'd be there in the waiting room, ready to greet my blank stare with a smile and my question with the same answer: "Groundhog Day."

February 2, 2005
Groundhog Day
Myrtle Beach, South Carolina

Daniel decided we both needed some time away, so after making arrangements to have his parents watch Sarah and Noah, he talked to one of his college friends, my brother Kyle, and two of his golfing buddies, and set up a mini-vacation for all of us.

For several months after the jump attempt, I had struggled with extreme tiredness. My friend Robin recommended Usana Health Pack supplements to me. I tried them and discovered that they dramatically improved my energy levels. Where I had found it hard to get out of bed previously, I now felt energetic enough to enjoy the vacation activities.

While the men went golfing, my sister-in-law, Sarah, and I went shopping. Have I mentioned that my husband loves golf? Not just loves it—lives for it. If he has a spare moment, he's on a course. A few times it's been the source of aggravation, and sometimes I outright hated it, but on this day I didn't care. He was having a good time and needed a break.

At the end of the day Sarah and I met the men at a place near the hotel with plans to go out to dinner. One look at Daniel and I knew dinner wasn't going to happen. After coming off the golf course, he, my brother, and their friends had ordered a few drinks to celebrate. Daniel had not eaten breakfast, so the alcohol had made him one sick puppy.

I took him for a walk along the boardwalk, thinking the night air might help him. During the walk he broke down and started crying. I'd never seen him like this before. He started talking about everything—the months of trying to figure out how to help me, the struggle to keep his job, to keep up with the house and take care of the kids while worrying about me, the fear when I'd gone to the bridge that day, the press, the pressure, the endless days and nights of trying to be strong, trying to be calm, trying to be a rock I could lean on. He'd finally reached the end of himself and it all came pouring out.

In between trying to explain how hard it had been on him, he kept apologizing for getting drunk. I don't know which broke my heart more. I'm not sure if it is proper to say that anyone "deserves" to get plastered, but in Dan's case, I think even the staunchest of religious souls could grant him this one instance of overimbibing and letting out all the pent-up pain.

Finally, one of our friends came and helped me get Daniel back to our hotel room.

Neither of us got much sleep that night. Dan continued to be sick well into the next day, taking up temporary quarters on the bathroom floor just in case. Bless his heart, Daniel was even worried about falling asleep for fear he had alcohol poisoning. I couldn't sleep because everything he said kept rolling over and over in my mind.

Somehow Dan had held together through it all and, even more importantly, he'd held our family together. I sat at the hotel window and marveled at the second chance I'd been given. I could have died that day on the bridge, probably would have died, but one event after another lined up so perfectly that I was still here. I'd get to see my children grow up, fall in love, and get married someday. I'd find my way back to happiness again.

If Daniel hadn't seen me go by, if State Police Officer Les Boldt hadn't been at that post office at that moment of the day and if he hadn't ignored orders, if Sergeant Bill Morgan hadn't been sitting in that particular parking lot, if a hidden ledge hadn't broken my downward momentum, if Officer Boldt had fumbled with his seatbelt or stumbled as he ran—I'd have plunged two hundred feet into the Fox River and my family would be grieving my loss.

I heard Daniel groan and started to go to him, but then I heard him sigh heavily and realized he was still dozing there on the bathroom floor.

I looked out the window at the night sky and settled back into the chair. I knew the reason so many things went right that day was because of nine women who refused to stop praying for me and because so many in my church, perhaps people I'd never know, also held me up to the Lord.

The strength to find my way back to normal wasn't just in the medications I took or the therapy I underwent, or even in the ECT. It was all those things combined with a husband who loved me enough to fight for me, stand by my side, and believe I could be me again. It was also friends who brought cards and meals and cleaned my house, women who took care of my children and offered many words of encouragement, and a faith in a God bigger than depression or rape or drugs or injury or pain.

We don't come back from depression alone, which is why depression can be so difficult. It convinces you that no one cares, that no one understands, and that there is no hope. The truth is people do care, and even when they don't understand, they still love you. And the truth is, there is hope.

As I sat in that hotel room pondering the path of my life, I realized something important had happened that night on the boardwalk, walking with Daniel and watching him fall apart.

While he was breaking down, I had remained stable and steadfast. For the first time in a very long time, I felt strong again.

When we arrived home from Myrtle Beach, Noah got sick with a barky cough. We took him to the doctor, who diagnosed an upper respiratory virus. Since Noah's throat had closed up, he was admitted to the hospital and put on a breathing machine. It was so difficult to see my baby in such misery, but my health wouldn't allow me to stay with him. Daniel stayed at the hospital the two nights and didn't get much sleep. At home, caring for Sarah, I tossed and turned as well, wondering when I could have my baby home with me.

Noah came home the third day, but the homecoming was tempered with the news that my biological father's father had passed away. I decided to attend the funeral. Once again the stress was beginning to snowball, and by the time I got back from the funeral and met with my doctor at a regularly scheduled appointment, I was starting to sink back down into depression. This is one of the hardest things about depression. You start to feel better and then something triggers it again, usually stress. There are biochemical reasons for this, but many people don't understand. It just appears to them that you are refusing to get well. Instead of understanding about Daniel, Noah, and then my grandfather, the doctor yelled at me, telling me that trying to kill myself wasn't going to get me to heaven.

His anger sent me spiraling downward once again.

When I got home from the doctor's office, Robin called to chat. The moment she heard my voice she said, "I'm coming over."

When she arrived a few minutes later, she asked me to take a walk with her. As we walked, she probed me with questions until the stress that had been accumulating came pouring out— the ECT, the memory loss, Dan's breakdown, Noah's illness, my grandfather's death, the doctor yelling at me. I told her that I'd finally figured out that I could be strong going *through* things, but afterward I tended to crumple. That's okay if you're only going through one or two things at a time, but so much stress all at once would just drag me down too far.

"You're not going to go back down, Tina." Robin squeezed my hand. "I know it seems overwhelming right now, and you're worried that this flood of feelings is going to sweep you back down into that dark hole, but it's not. You're beyond that now. You are getting stronger. You can handle this."

"It feels the same," I replied as I brushed away the tears.

"It's not," Robin insisted. "Listen to me, Tina. There's a reason for everything. You'll see. There's a reason for this and it's all good. You know the Word of God. All things work together for the good of those that love him. It's not that God wanted all this bad stuff to happen in your life—nothing could be further from the truth. This is not a perfect world, and bad things happen to wonderful people. If it were a perfect world, then it would be heaven. But God promises to take every tear, every heartache, and use it, ultimately, for good in your life if you'll hand it over to him."

Her words did encourage me a little, but when I went to see my counselor the next day, I still felt it was important to share with her all that had transpired. Her reaction was not quite what I expected. She got angry about my doctor's reaction, so angry, in fact, that she wrote him a letter.

Two days later he called me to his office and apologized. I told him that the doctor who administered the Botox injections in my back (Botox freezes the muscle and helps alleviate pain) suggested that I try Cymbalta, a new medication for depression. My doctor agreed to put me on it. Within two weeks of taking the Cymbalta, I knew I was feeling well enough to stop the ECT.

After eight months of treatments, no more ECT. Initially I was supposed to have only six treatments, but because of the severity of the depressive symptoms, the doctor ended up prescribing twenty-two, which took quite a toll on my body. Each time I went for a treatment, I came home sore from the spasms, I didn't feel like eating, my temples hurt, and I had headaches.

Finally, there were no more Groundhog Days, no more trying to remember whom I had talked to the day before the treatment, no more little notes all over the house to remind me of things I didn't want to forget, no more using maps to get to the grocery store. I was on the road to recovery, and for the first time since the jump, I could see my life coming back together—until my sister Whitney showed up one day to visit me.

"I showed Dad the article about your jump."

I spun around, shocked, as she sat there calmly informing me that she was still in contact with our stepfather. "You still talk to him?"

She shrugged. "Sure. He was the man who raised us. He's the only father I've ever known."

I dropped down in the chair next to her. "He's also the man who sexually molested me. He beat up our mother. How could you even *want* to talk to him?"

"Look, he made a mistake and apologized for it. How long are you going to hold it against him?"

It wasn't about holding anything against him. According to every therapist and counselor I'd talked to, I was supposed to forgive him for my own sense of well-being, and I had done that, but that didn't mean I had to let him come back into my life and mess it up again.

Daniel and I decided that I was feeling well enough to start taking care of Noah a little more. It was still very painful for me to lift him, but Deborah helped out, along with two neighbors, as we transitioned to having Noah back in our home during the day.

By April, between taking care of Noah, which meant lifting, bending, and stretching, and trying to do more housework, my back pain was getting much worse. I increased my pain medication substantially, and the doctor increased my Botox injections. When Marcia, a friend from church, offered to take Noah in the afternoons, I gratefully accepted her help.

In spite of the pain, I was determined to take care of my baby, my husband, and my house. I just had to find a way through the pain and keep it from triggering a depression episode again.

chapter twelve

Step into the Light

June 2005
Green Bay, Wisconsin

You need to write a book."

After sharing my story at a MOPS meeting one day, one of my friends came to me and uttered those simple words. They were words I couldn't shake off. They stayed with me day and night.

Did I have a story to tell? The more I thought about it, the more strongly I felt that telling my story was not only something that I should do, it was something that I needed to do.

Robin and I started talking about what such a project would entail. We went to bookstores and looked at other true-life drama books as well as how-to books on writing. I started outlining my life and researching events and people, digging back into memories that had grown vague to substantiate the actual truth.

The further we went, the more we knew we weren't up to the task. If this book was going to be written, God would have to pull it all together.

Robin and I had attended a Beth Moore conference. Before going, Robin and another friend wrote Beth a letter explaining how much her Bible studies had helped me and a little bit about my experiences, as well as my hope to write a book. We were sitting in the audience when suddenly Beth said, "Where is Tina Zahn?"

Slowly, I raised my hand.

"Stand up, Tina. Please."

I stood, dragging Robin up with me. As soon as I was on my feet, she smiled at me. "Child, how am I going to get you up here so that I can give you a hug?"

I couldn't believe she was singling me out, but her next words changed everything for me.

"Tina, I want you to know that all these women here are going to be praying for you." Everyone started clapping and it was all I could do not to run from the place in tears; I was just so overwhelmed.

I went home with a renewed sense of purpose. At a follow-up leadership conference, which Beth Moore organized, one woman said that every day she asked the Lord a simple question: "Lord, what do *you* want me to do today?"

I began praying this prayer every day. I knew I wanted to write a book, but I needed help.

When I arrived home from the Beth Moore conference, I found a letter from my stepfather waiting for me on the counter. I stared at the envelope. Was I strong enough to read this without getting swamped by old fears and fresh pain?

Slowly I ripped it open and, taking a deep breath, started reading. It was a chatty little letter that made one thing perfectly clear. He wanted to be back in my life. I left the letter on the table for Daniel to read when he got home.

"It sounds like he's finally recognizing his mistakes and trying to change his life," I told my husband as he read the letter. "But is what he wrote true?"

"There's only one way we can know for sure," Daniel replied, folding the letter and handing it back to me. "And that's to meet with him like he asked."

The meeting with my stepfather didn't resolve any of our issues, but he did promise not to contact me again. The good news was, I hadn't fallen apart. I hadn't been overwhelmed by my emotions. I was definitely getting better, bit by bit, every day.

One day, reading through a magazine, I came across an ad for Carol Kent's Speak Up seminar in Milwaukee. I knew I needed to go to this conference to learn how to share my story more effectively with others, but there were obstacles in the way. I needed someone to drive me, since I still couldn't drive myself. And who would have the time to do that?

Once again Robin came through for me, agreeing to drive me to the conference, stay with me while I attended, and bring me home again.

The prayer team at the one-year anniversary of the jump.

The prayer team that prayed throughout the writing of the book.

July 19, 2005
The Anniversary

On the one-year anniversary of my jump off Tower Drive Bridge, we held an anniversary party for all the women who had been praying so faithfully, first for my healing before Noah was born, then my healing after the jump, and now for a book that was little more than an idea.

Cassie, who was hosting the party, asked everyone to write their feelings on a card or letter to give me at the party. Two of the women showed up with the same card, which quoted Jeremiah 29:11—"'For I know the plans I have for you,' declares the Lord, 'plans to prosper you and not to harm you, plans to give you hope and a future.'"

As I sat among these women, my heart couldn't help but be overwhelmed by their love and prayers. Without them, who could say what might have happened that day on the bridge? I had no doubt that their prayers brought about all the miracles that fell into place that day to save my life. Did they understand the importance of what they had done out of friendship? Maybe they did and maybe they didn't, but I knew I would never be able to repay the debt I owed them. They had given something more precious than all the gold in the world. They had given me their love.

July 22, 2005
Carol Kent's Speak Up seminar
Milwaukee, Wisconsin

When Robin and I arrived at the conference, we stood in line to register, chatting casually with some of the other women in line. As we neared the front of the line, I was talking about the problems we were facing as we tried to write this book. "We need a writer, someone who knows how to take this and make it a book," I said.

But I had no clue how to find such a person. The lady in front of me finished and walked away, so I stepped up to the person sitting behind the registration desk. "Tina Zahn and Robin Fischer," I said.

As the woman pulled up the paperwork we'd filled out and sent in, she glanced up at me. "Welcome! My name is Shirley. I think I know someone who might be able to help you. Let me check and get back to you."

Thanking her, I filed it away as a nice gesture; I finished registering and went on in to the conference. Immediately swept up into the program, all thoughts of the book vanished.

I was supposed to come up with three short speeches, each three minutes long with a spiritual application. The best I could do under such pressure was come up with one.

When my turn came I was shaking like a leaf. I stood up and walked over to the microphone and faced the audience, their faces blurring as I struggled with my nervousness.

"On July 19 of last year, I grabbed my car keys off a counter, got in my car, and headed for the Tower Drive Bridge. I was coming into Green Bay when all of a sudden I saw my husband's Durango coming toward me on the other side of the highway. I hit the gas, soon going over a hundred miles an hour. My next memory is that of a police car chasing me, but I was determined to get to the bridge and not let him stop me.

"Reports say that I got to the bridge before the state trooper. I didn't think twice and jumped off headfirst. The state trooper, Les Boldt, grabbed my right wrist and hung on with both hands. Both of our lives hung in the balance two hundred feet above the Fox River. I had hit a ledge, which broke my fall. Police stated that if I had not hit that ledge, the force of gravity would have taken both of us over. Sixteen seconds passed before the next police officer arrived. He grabbed my left wrist and hung on. More seconds passed before the third police officer arrived and the three of them hoisted me back over the concrete barrier.

"The dramatic rescue was captured by the state police car video camera. The tape showed Officer Boldt's feet leaving the ground as he lunged for me. The next day, that dramatic rescue hit the airways. Local news stations and national news media picked up the story, playing it for several days. Officer Les Boldt was featured on several local and national stations and praised for going beyond the call of duty.

"Officer Boldt stated that he only had one thing on his mind as he hung on until more help arrived. 'I'm not letting you go,' he told me as we struggled there on the bridge. 'I've got you.' He told one reporter that all he was thinking was that he had to get me back on the other side, to hold on and not

Tina with Wanda Dyson.

let me drop. No other thought entered his mind but that of saving my life.

"In the same way that the state trooper said, 'I'm not letting you go,' so God also has us in his grip and will never let go of us. In Joshua 1:5 it says, 'As I was with Moses, so I will be with you; I will never leave you nor forsake you.'"

Tears streamed from my eyes as I finished speaking, but I was no longer shaking.

Jennie Dimkoff, Carol Kent's sister, locked eyes with me as I started to step away from the microphone. "Who sent you here?" she asked.

I swallowed hard. If I told her the truth, would she understand?

"The Lord," I replied.

The following week, I received an email from Greg Johnson,

a literary agent. Shirley had come through! I called Greg and spoke at some length about my story.

"I have a couple of writers that you can choose from," he told me. "You pick the one that you think is best suited for this book."

The first writer I called to interview was Wanda Dyson. After speaking for an hour, we agreed to talk again the next day. After that second call, I knew she was the woman who was meant to write this story—that she could understand what pushed me to the bridge and what had brought me to this point. I called Greg back and told him, "No need to look anymore. We have our writer."

Ever since I was a child, playing in my grandparents' pond, I've been in love with the water. Not long after Sarah was born, I came up with the idea that we needed a hobby that would include the whole family. I chose boating and, while Daniel didn't know a thing about boats or boating, he was willing to learn. He found a boat on eBay that he liked, and we drove all the way to Fargo, North Dakota, to check it out. The owners had a sick child in the hospital and needed to sell it to help pay medical expenses. When we pulled up in their driveway, we discovered that the boat was the same color as Daniel's SUV. We took that as a good sign, bought the boat, and hauled our new purchase home.

Each summer prior to my getting pregnant with Noah, we'd put that boat in the water and take advantage of every nice day to be out there. When I was finally well enough to get back on the boat, we were eager to resume our hobby. It was a summer celebration each time we loaded Sarah and Noah into the boat and motored away from the dock into open water, the sun on our shoulders, the wind blowing freedom.

I had my church activities and women's groups, the family had boating together, and Daniel had golf. Golf is Daniel's passion. He's won many tournaments, including the Beat the Pro tournament. The problem was that over the years I'd come to see golf as the enemy. It took Daniel away from me for hours, and I resented every moment he spent out on the course. Every time he picked up those golf clubs, I felt abandoned.

One Sunday in August, Sarah was going to sing a song on Sunday morning as part of her vacation Bible school program at Green Bay Community Church. I asked Dan, who was still attending St. Mark's Lutheran, to please come to my church and support Sarah. He showed up, but as soon as Sarah finished her song, he was gone—heading for the golf course.

I was crushed.

Later I called one of my closest friends with a "woe is me, the golf widow" tale. Rather than feed into my pity party, she gently reminded me that Dan needed his passion just as much as I needed mine. I was constantly going to women's ministry meetings, Bible classes, retreats, and conferences. How would I feel if Daniel resented that and felt abandoned each time I went?

Gulp. She had a point. I still wasn't sure that I spent as much time on my passion as he spent on his, but it was a sign of progress that I was willing to see my feelings for what they were and bring them to heel.

Now if I could just bring some other emotions to heel as easily. It was a task I wasn't sure I was up to.

Niagara Falls vacation in 1995.

Dan, Tina, and Sarah (1 year old) in Door County, Wisconsin.

Noah Zahn
at age 18 months.

Sarah and Noah in October 2005.

Tina, Noah, Dan, and Sarah celebrating Noah's second birthday.

chapter thirteen

Beauty out of the Ashes

October 2005

W hen my church announced that it was going to schedule baptisms for anyone who had made a decision
for Christ, I knew I had to sign up. The baptisms were planned
for the sixteenth of October. On that Sunday morning, I was
the last of fifteen people to step into the baptismal pool and
give my story of how my faith journey had made a difference
in my life.

I talked about God reaching out from the heavens and saving me on that bridge and about how he'd given me a second
chance—to live to see another day—and also a chance to experience what it was like to have a good and kind Father. Then
the pastor lowered me into the water.

When I came up, wiping the water from my eyes, he looked

straight at me and said, "Now, isn't this better than the Fox River?"

I giggled. Indeed it was. Had I jumped off that bridge and landed in the Fox River, I wouldn't have come up again, alive to everything God had for me. It would have been certain death.

But I was alive—and looking forward to everything my heavenly Father planned for my future.

During this time I was studying all I could about emotional and spiritual healing. One day I came across a suggestion in a workbook: the instant you start feeling fearful, do not delay. Immediately ask God to help you. I copied the suggestion down on a note card and carried it in my pocket.

I was still on Lorazepam and hated the way this medication made me groggy, so I made a deal with myself. Each time I felt anxious, instead of taking a pill, I'd pray. Within two weeks, I went from six tablets a day down to one a day. My prayer life shot up to a whole new level.

In spite of his promise not to contact me again, on October 18 I received another letter from my stepfather. He was trying to ease his way back into my life. This time I was more prepared and much further along in my healing. Just the day before I'd heard a former police officer who specialized in domestic violence talking about his new book, which among other things presented the profile of the abuser. He described my stepfather down to the last detail, calling this sort of man a "master manipulator."

The police officer explained how abusers will usually go into professions that put them in a position of authority and power, like law enforcement or the military. They consider their word as the final authority; they are jealous and possessive, and when it comes to relationships, they swoop in, sweep a woman off her feet, and get involved quickly to avoid giving her time to back out. It made me think about how my mom once told me that the day she married my stepfather, she was standing on the steps of the courthouse and felt a sudden urge to run, but she needed someone to help her raise her children.

The master manipulator will isolate you, cutting you off from friends and family. He is cruel to children. The author warned women that if they ever found themselves swept up in a relationship with a man that they even suspected might be rushing them into a relationship, to look into his background, especially civil and court records.

This detective had been dealing with domestic abuse at all levels for more than twenty-five years, and throughout the interview, I sat transfixed in front of the radio.

Domestic abuse is terrifying to the watching children, but churches are hesitant to get involved because in most cases they are not equipped to deal with it. Abuse is an anger problem, not a marriage counseling problem. Most pastors are trained to work toward reconciliation and don't always think about the safety of the wife and children.

Standing there with my stepfather's letter in my hand, I knew that this time I had to completely cut all ties with him. He had to know that I was too strong for him to manipulate or intimidate ever again.

I picked up the phone and called Sergeant Bill Morgan. Since the day of the jump he had become a close family friend and had told me many times that if I needed him for anything to just call. When I got him on the phone, I explained the situation.

"Bill, I just got another letter from my stepfather. I need to put an end to this, so I need to meet with him."

"Do you think you're ready?" he asked.

"I know I am. I just want to ask a favor of you, if you don't mind."

"Ask away."

I smiled, knowing he meant it to the core of that big heart of his. "I want to invite him to lunch and I want to explain to him that he is to never contact me again, but just to make sure I'm safe, in case his temper gets out of control, I'd like you to go with me."

"Consider it done. Would you like me to wear my uniform?" he asked with a deep rumbling laugh that would warm people right down to their toes.

I couldn't help laughing in return. "I doubt that will be necessary. Just you being there should be enough."

On the day of the meeting, I drove to the restaurant where we would meet my stepfather. Daniel and Sergeant Morgan were already there, waiting for me in the parking lot. "Are you ready?" Bill asked.

"Yes and no," I answered truthfully. "Let's just do this." In reality I was feeling sick to my stomach and shaking like a leaf, but I had a deep-seated resolve, so I took a deep breath, opened the door to the restaurant, and walked in.

My stepfather was already there, smiling as we walked up to the table.

"You know my husband, but I'd like to introduce a friend of ours, Sergeant Bill Morgan."

My stepfather was clearly unhappy with Bill's presence. "Is he here to intimidate me or something?"

"No," I told him as we all sat down. "He's here at my request because I want you to understand just how serious I am. You promised me that you wouldn't make contact with me again. You broke that promise."

"I needed to talk to you." He started crying, talking about suicide and how he didn't have anyone in his life. He blamed this on his parents and everyone else who, in his mind, simply abandoned him without just cause.

I sat there, trying to drink my orange juice as I listened to him. I knew that my stepfather would never take any responsibility for the stream of broken relationships in his past. I also knew that it was not my burden to carry. I had to get well; I needed to be surrounded by healthy people. Finally, I couldn't stand any more. "Just don't contact me again," I said.

Ignoring me, he started to launch into another diatribe, a stream of words that made no real sense but was designed to manipulate my emotions.

Bill Morgan leaned across the table. "Do you understand what Tina has said? You are not to contact her again."

Finally, I stood up. "I have to go now. Don't contact me again," I repeated.

I staggered out of the restaurant and into the parking lot, trying to assimilate all the emotions raging through me. My stepfather seemed so pitiful, so lost. I knew it was all part of the manipulation game and that I shouldn't let it get to me, but still, there was something so sad about it all. "I feel so bad for him," I confessed to Bill and Dan.

"Don't," Bill said as he gave me a reassuring hug. "He'll be fine."

"Thanks for coming," I replied softly, my thoughts as scattered as paper in a windstorm.

"Anytime."

After Bill drove off, Dan walked me to my car. "Well, one thing's for sure."

"What's that?"

"I finally saw what you've been trying to tell me for years about your stepfather."

I tried to smile, thrilled that he could understand that I hadn't been crazy after all.

He gave me a quick hug. "I have to get back to work."

"Can't we get something to eat?" I asked Dan. "Maybe at Subway? I'm not quite ready to be alone yet."

He glanced at his watch. "Sure."

At the sub shop, Dan ordered our lunch while I went into the bathroom. I was so confused, trying to remind myself that nothing my stepfather said was real.

When I got back to the table, Dan said, "I need to get back to work."

I glanced down and realized that he had ordered only my lunch. "Aren't you going to eat?" I asked, hoping he'd say yes.

"I don't have time. Maybe I'll grab something later. Are you going to be okay?"

"I'll be fine," I assured him, but in truth, I wasn't fine at all. I had talked myself into believing that I was just going to walk in there with Dan and Bill Morgan and tell my stepfather to leave me alone and then it would all be over. End of story. Instead, my stepfather had played on my sympathy. When that didn't seem to work, he spouted off one story after another about my family until my thoughts were a mass of confusion. I didn't know up from down, what was truth and what wasn't.

I knew I wasn't ready to go home and be alone. I pulled out my cell phone and called Robin.

"Hey. You busy?"

"I'm on that wallpapering job at the house at Lake Largo, so I'm up to my elbows in paste. What's up?"

"I met with my stepfather."

There was a slight pause before she said, "You know how to get here. Come spend some time with me."

"You sure?"

"Positive," she replied firmly. "I'll see you in a few minutes."

While Robin hung wallpaper, I handed her whatever materials or tools she asked for while I told her about the meeting with my stepfather. We chatted about all the different things he said, trying to guess what was fact and what was fiction. By the time we'd gone through it all, I felt calm and able to deal with whatever might happen next.

The ECT had given me a boost out of the deepest, darkest hole imaginable, and after trying one medication after another, we finally found one that helped me recover from the depression. So we had cleared the most obvious weeds in my life to a manageable ground level. Now we needed to kill the roots, or else the depression and its symptoms would reappear at some point.

I knew that digging at the roots of my angst would be painful but necessary. A few people had recommended a program called Reiki, and I tried it for a while. Reiki is a Japanese practice of meditation and the use of a "spirit guide" to reduce stress and promote emotional healing. The idea behind Reiki is that you will tap into the life force energy of a "Higher Wisdom" or "Higher Power." During the session, you are to call on a spirit "light" or "guide" to walk back through traumatic events with you. While the practitioner tried to make me comfortable by telling me to think of this "light" or "spirit guide" as Jesus, I just couldn't be involved in practices that were in direct opposition to my faith.

Then I heard about Cleansing Streams Ministries and their extensive program of healing specifically designed to help people overcome past traumas. I signed up and went through the course.

On the front of the workbook is Jeremiah 29:11: "'For I know the plans I have for you,' declares the LORD, 'plans to prosper you and not to harm you, plans to give you hope and a future.'" That Scripture had crossed my path many times since the day I jumped off the Tower Drive Bridge and had come to mean *hope* to me in so many ways. I knew after reading that Scripture I had to go through the class. They warned us on the first night that it wouldn't always be easy and that we would get out of the course only as much as we were willing to put into it. The study included a workbook, three small books, two CDs, and a heavy reading schedule.

Sure enough, the class was emotionally demanding and several people dropped out. But for those of us who made it through, it was life changing. We confronted myriad topics including abuse, guilt, shame, condemnation, rejection, unforgiveness, fear, bitterness, and depression. I walked out of every class feeling as if someone had recharged my battery.

When the Christmas season rolled around, Daniel and I took the kids and Daniel's parents to the annual parade and then out to the tree farm to get our Christmas tree. The weather was clear, cold, and crisp. Children were running from tree to tree, dodging adults and admonitions to be careful, and the holiday spirit infected everyone with a sense of playful anticipation.

"This one, Daddy. I like this one!"

"No. This one is better."

"Look at this one, Mommy."

Daniel was just transferring Noah from his hip to the ground when Howard stepped out from between two tall evergreens, scratching his head.

"What's the matter, Dad?" Daniel asked.

"I lost my tree."

I couldn't help laughing as Howard walked off to find another "perfect" Christmas tree, while Sarah followed to make sure he didn't lose another one.

As I heard my own laughter, I reflected on the last Christmas when, still mired in depression, I'd cried over not feeling as though I had a family. Now, as I stood in the cold, holding Noah's hand and inhaling the sweet smell of pine, I knew that my family had been here all along. They had loved, supported, and encouraged me in every way they knew how, and when they failed, it wasn't because they didn't care. Maybe it was because they cared too much. I had spent so many years looking back at what wasn't right in my childhood that I had been missing what was right with my present.

As a child consumed with pain, I felt I needed my mom to be the perfect June Cleaver mother with all the right answers at all the right times to eradicate my pain. The reality was that my mother had married young and soon found herself divorced with three children. Then she was trapped in a second marriage because she was afraid of not being able to take care of her children by herself. Instead of seeking a better way out of a tough situation, she found herself in an even worse situation: she became the mother of five children and the wife of an abusive husband. How do you blame someone for handling the pain handed to her in the only way she knew how? Denial was the only method of coping she knew. Heaven knows I'd made plenty of my own mistakes trying to handle my pain. People generally do whatever they can to make pain go away, even temporarily. But when we know better, we can do better.

I don't know anyone who thinks he or she had the perfect mother or father. I doubt Sarah and Noah will think I was the perfect mother, but I can only do my best for them and pray I do the important things right from this day forward.

Sarah came running back, breathless with excitement, her eyes sparkling with joy. "Mommy! Look at this tree! Isn't it perfect?" She grabbed my hand, pulling me closer to the tree that Daniel was carrying.

It wasn't exactly perfect; nothing in life is. But with garland and lights and all the love this family would lavish on it, it would be perfect for us.

"Yes, Sarah, it is perfect."

chapter fourteen

I Lift Up My Eyes

For too many years I tried to fix myself. When I had a problem, I took care of it. With anything and everything, I tried to do life on my own. Then came a day when all my efforts left me exhausted, broken, despondent, and empty. I looked out the window that day and asked God, "What next?"

When we reach the end of ourselves, God is there. Healing doesn't come in a day or an hour or a session. It doesn't come with one pill or one bottle of pills, with one doctor or one treatment. And it doesn't always come easily for those of us with decades of pain buried deep beneath the surface. But healing can come. You can't give up.

I did give up for a time, but not because I wanted to. I simply ran out of strength to keep on going.

When my brother Kyle was being interviewed for this book, he was asked about his favorite memory of me when we were children. He said when he was about seven or eight, there were seven people in a house with only one bathroom. He and I used to argue all the time because he thought I spent too much time hogging the shower. One night he decided he'd had enough and kept pounding on the door, yelling at me. He said I opened the door, cool as you please, and punched him, giving him a bloody nose.

He laughed and said, "For a while, my sister lost that strong, persistent, never-give-up personality of hers, but it's back. She's back."

And I am. Not because I found that old strength and used it, but because I found a new strength.

I have a husband who wouldn't give up on me, even when he could barely find the energy to get through one more hour. And I have a brother who never turned his back on me. I have Deborah, Howard, and Greatgram who did everything they could to love and care for me, even when I wasn't the least bit lovable. I had friends that gave more than I could ever ask or expect, more than I could possibly repay.

I had people I didn't even know encouraging me and praying for me—clerks and waitresses, receptionists and pharmacists. They'd hear about me and when they'd see me come in, they'd come over to tell me that they were praying for me. That was always so astounding.

I had music. I can't even begin to tell you how important music was to my healing. Whenever I started to feel myself sliding backward even an inch, I'd turn on the music and it would lift me back up.

But the most important ingredient in my healing was God. He didn't do some kind of modern-day miracle and heal me in the blink of an eye, but he was there holding my hand while we went from one medication to another until we found the one that worked for me. He showed up in the faces of good doctors and kind nurses. He was there for every Groundhog Day as I struggled through the memory loss after each ECT. He gave me the strength to face therapy and self-examination and the fortitude to go back over my past and relive each and every painful memory. Then he gave me the power to take the pain out of those memories and put them to rest.

You'll find God in church, but you'll also find him in the hands and hearts of the people around you every day, people reaching out to let you know they care. And in those times, when you want to push people away and pull the covers over your head, God is still there. He knows the plans he has for you, plans to prosper you and give you hope—and a future.

You may say, "You don't understand. I don't believe in God." That's okay. He believes in you. And even if you can't believe he's there, ask him to help you anyway. What do you have to lose? Just try praying, "God, I don't even know if you exist. I don't know if you care. But I'm willing to open my mind to that possibility and I'd like to ask you to help me."

I lift up my eyes to the hills—where does my help come from? My help comes from the Lord, the Maker of heaven and earth.

Psalm 121:1–2

211

What I wanted more than anything in my life was to be accepted for who I was and loved unconditionally. But before I could believe that anyone loved me, I had to learn that I was worthy of love. I tried behaving in ways I thought people wanted me to behave. I tried to be compliant, submissive, obedient, and "good." I didn't speak up or speak out. I held on to secrets until they choked the life out of me. But all the while, I hated hiding behind a mask, knowing that I wasn't letting anyone see the real me for fear of more rejection.

The mask is off now. The secrets are out, and everything I'd feared hasn't materialized. On the contrary, I have a better relationship now with Deborah and Greatgram and Howard than I ever expected to have. We can sit at the table over coffee and talk for hours, and there's no tension. We hug and there is no resentment hovering beneath the surface. I can genuinely love them for who they are, and they love me right back.

I've stepped out into the light, and as the shadows of the past disappear, I find that the little girl I thought no one loved had been loved after all. God cherished her from the start, and he continues to do so. I realized that there was nothing I could do to make God love me any more, and nothing I could do to make him love me less. The same is true for you.

Depression is a liar. It will tell you whatever it can to keep you embroiled in the darkness.

But there is joy in the light.

There is hope in the future.

And there is someone loving you every step of the way.

Facts and Figures

Sexual Abuse in Children: What to Look For . . .

Clinical manifestations of sexual abuse can include: Vaginal, penile, or rectal pain; redness of area or a discharge with or without bleeding; chronic painful urination; constipation.

Behavioral manifestations can include: sexualized activity with peers, animals, or objects; seductive behavior; age-inappropriate sexual knowledge and curiosity; suicide gestures; fear of an individual or place; nightmares; sleep disorders; regression; aggression; withdrawn behavior; post-traumatic stress disorder; poor self-esteem; depression; running away; self-mutilation; anxiety; fire setting; multiple personalities; somatization (multiple recurring pains and pseudo-neurological symptoms appearing in adolescence and in full criteria by age 30); phobias; prostitution or sexual promiscuity; drug abuse; eating disorders.

Richard E. Behram, Robert M. Kliegman, Ann Arvin, *Nelson Textbook of Pediatrics,* 15th ed. (Philadelphia: Saunders 2001); Arnold Kaplan, M.D., Benjamin Sadock, M.D., and Jack Greeb, M.D., *Synopsis of Psychiatry: Behavioral Sciences in Clinical Psychiatry,* 7th ed. (Hagerstown, MD: Williams and Wilkins, 1999)

Facts about Sexual Assault against Children

1. Child sexual abuse is not a rare occurrence. It is estimated that approximately one in every four females and one in every six males experience some form of sexual exploitation as children.

2. Eighty-five percent of these children are molested by someone they know, i.e., family members, relatives, neighbors, or family friends.

3. The role the offender plays in the child's life may be vital, that is, he or she may be a close family member or someone in the position of trust. The abuse occurring will be very confusing to the child because of the secrecy, shame, lies, and isolation that follow. The child wants the abusive behavior to stop but does not want to lose the hope of protection and caring that are his or her right.

4. Sexual abuse of children is an act of violence, even if there are no physical injuries. Children who are sexual abuse victims are denied a childhood, denied a loving and nurturing relationship of trust, and exploited and betrayed by a person who is in a position of authority and trust.

5. Children do not have the explicit sexual knowledge necessary to describe phenomena they have not experienced and do not have the cognitive capacities to make up stories of sexual abuse. If children lie about sexual abuse, it is most often to deny that it did occur in order to protect the offender and/or the family unit.

6. Child sexual abuse typically goes on for quite some time

before discovery. It is not confined to one child, but usually involves several children.

7. Adults often do not talk about child sexual abuse because of their own discomfort with the topic. If adults are not willing to talk about the abuse, the child will probably feel there is something to be ashamed of, that it is dirty and just too awful to talk about. This attitude will only serve to increase the child's feelings of guilt and shame and of being abnormal, compounding the child's problems.

The Rape Advocacy Program
17 West Prentiss St. • Iowa City, IA 52240 • http://www.jeonet.com/city/rvap.htm

Sexual Assault Center
www.sace.ab.ca/Myths.htm

Profile of an Abuser

- Uncontrolled temper
- Poor coping skills
- Unreasonably demanding
- Extremely jealous and possessive
- Extreme mood swings
- Denial that abuse occurs
- Expressing remorse and begging for forgiveness with seemingly loving gestures
- Intense fear of abandonment
- Threats of violence
- Inability to respect interpersonal boundaries

- A need for power and control that can drive the abuser into positions of authority, including law enforcement or the military
- Controlling and masterfully manipulative
- Blaming the victim or others for the behavior
- Often a hard worker and good provider
- Reckless and indulging in dangerous sexual behavior

The Broken Spirits Network
www.brokenspirits.com

Domestic Violence and the Courtroom
American Judges Association • http://aja.ncsc.dni.us/index.html

Abuse 101
Lifted Hearts Network • http://abuse101.com

Feeling like a Victim

Children who have been sexually abused feel many different and often overwhelming emotions including:

- *Fear*—of the abuser, of causing trouble, of losing adults important to them, of being taken away from home, of being "different."
- *Anger*—at the abuser, at other adults around them who did not protect them, at themselves (feeling as if they caused trouble).
- *Isolation*—because "something is wrong with me," because they feel alone in their experience, because they have trouble talking about the abuse.
- *Sadness*—about having something taken from them, about

losing a part of themselves, about growing up too fast, about being betrayed by someone they trusted.

- *Guilt*—for not being able to stop the abuse, for believing they "consented" to the abuse, for "telling" if they told, for keeping the secret if they did not tell.
- *Shame*—about being involved in the experience, about their body's response to the abuse.
- *Confusion*—because they may still love the abuser, because their feelings change all the time.

In addition, they may also suffer from depression, numbness, irritability, and hopelessness.

These feelings may manifest in the following ways:

- Nightmares
- Difficulty sleeping
- Memory loss
- Eating disturbances
- Difficulty trusting
- Decreased concentration
- Difficulty being alone or with people

Victim Assistance Unit
www.gov.calgary.ab.ca/police/inside/victim.html

American Academy of Experts in Traumatic Stress—Surviving the Pain
Barbara Bogorad, Psy. D. A.B.P.P.,
Founder and former director, Sexual Abuse Recovery Program, South Oaks Hospital, New York

Child Trauma Academy
Houston, Texas
www.childtrauma.org

Depression

Depression is more than just feeling blue or down. Some people liken depression to a black curtain of despair coming down on their lives. Most have no energy and can't concentrate. Others may feel irritable all the time for no apparent reason. Symptoms may vary from person to person, but if the feelings interfere with a person's daily life, he or she may be clinically depressed. Depression is a serious problem that affects all aspects of a person's life. It isn't a sign of personal weakness or failure. It's a sign that treatment is needed.

Most people who have gone through one episode of depression will have another one.

Know the Facts about Depression

- Approximately 18.8 million American adults aged 18 and older suffer from a depressive disorder in a given year.
- Nearly twice as many women as men are affected by a depressive disorder each year. These figures translate to more than 12.4 million women.
- In 2000 nearly 30,000 people died by suicide in the United States.
- More than 90 percent of those who killed themselves had a diagnosable depressive disorder.
- Nearly 74 percent of Americans who seek help for depression or symptoms of depression will go to a primary care physician rather than a mental health professional.

Symptoms of Depression

- Changes in appetite resulting in weight loss or gain
- Insomnia or oversleeping
- Loss of energy or increased fatigue
- Feelings of worthlessness or inappropriate guilt
- Difficulty thinking, concentrating, or making decisions
- Thoughts of death or suicide, or attempts at suicide
- Agitation or slowing of body movements
- Low self-esteem

National Institute of Mental Health
www.nimh.nih.gov/publicat/depression.cfm

Brookhaven Hospital • 201 S Garnet Rd.
Tulsa, OK 74128 • 888-298-HOPE
www.brookhavenhospital.com

GlaxoSmithKline
www.depression.com

American Psychiatric Association
1000 Wilson Blvd. • Suite 825
Arlington, VA 22209
www.healthyminds.org

Postpartum Depression

Postpartum depression is a type of depression that affects about one in ten new mothers within the first year after she gives birth, usually appearing within the first two weeks after delivery.

PPD is a more serious type of depression and is different from the "baby blues," which involves milder symptoms and occurs in 70 to 80 percent of all new mothers. Usually baby blues develops three to four days after delivery, and the symptoms usually disappear after a couple of weeks. Symptoms of baby blues include mild depression, mood swings, irregular sleeping and eating patterns, anxiety, and difficulty concentrating.

PPD requires immediate medical attention. A woman suffering from PPD can experience delusions and hallucinations, exhibit bizarre behavior and feelings, and can be extremely agitated.

Who Is at Risk for PPD?

Factors in a mother's environment can increase the likelihood that she will develop postpartum depression. Detecting risk factors early is crucial to preventing PPD. In most cases PPD is preventable, and early identification can lead to early treatment that will keep the disorder from getting worse. When a pregnant woman has one or more of the following characteristics, she should be carefully watched for signs of postpartum depression after giving birth.

- A young or single mother
- History of mental illness or substance abuse
- Financial or marital difficulties or has experienced other stressful life events
- Previous pregnancy, birth, or postpartum difficulties
- Complications during labor and/or birth
- Low confidence as a parent
- Problems with a baby's health

- A major life change at the same time as the birth
- Lack of support or help with the baby

Symptoms of PPD

- Increased crying and irritability
- Hopelessness and sadness
- Uncontrollable mood swings
- Feeling overwhelmed or unable to cope
- Fear of harming the baby, her partner, or herself
- Fear of being alone
- Lack of interest in the baby or overly concerned for the baby
- Poor self-care
- Loss of interest or pleasure in activities
- Decreased energy and motivation
- Withdrawal or isolation from friends and family
- Inability to think clearly or make decisions
- Exhaustion or sluggishness
- Sleep and appetite disturbances not related to care of the baby
- Headaches, chest pains, hyperventilation, heart palpitations

Warning for Previous Sufferers of PPD

PPD can be significantly worse with each successive pregnancy. PPD peaks at three months after giving birth.

Electroconvulsive Therapy

Electroconvulsive therapy (ECT) is generally used in severely depressed patients for whom psychotherapy and medication have proved ineffective. It may also be considered as a treatment when there is an imminent risk of suicide, because often ECT has much quicker results than antidepressant remedies.

During ECT the patient is anesthetized with an intravenous injection of a barbiturate or other anesthetic. The muscles are temporarily paralyzed with the drug succinylcholine, which prevents the violent jerking motions that used to break bones during the therapy. In bilateral ECT, electrodes are placed above each temple. In unilateral ECT, the electrodes are placed above the temple of one side of the brain and in the middle of the forehead. An electrical current is then passed through the brain, inducing a grand mal seizure.

When the patient awakens, there may be headache, nausea, temporary confusion, and muscle stiffness. Many patients report loss of memory of events that occurred in the days, weeks, or months surrounding the ECT. Many of these memories may return although not always. Some patients have also reported that their short-term memory continues to be affected for months.

www.psycom.net/depression.central.ect.html

For Additional Help

4 Therapy Network
www.4therapy.com

American Academy of Experts in Traumatic Stress
368 Veterans Memorial Highway
Commack, NY 11725
www.aaets.org

American Psychiatric Association
1000 Wilson Blvd
Suite 1825
Arlington, VA 22209
703-907-7300
www.healthyminds.org

Brookhaven Mental Health Hospital
201 S Garnett Rd
Tulsa, OK 74128
888-298-HOPE
www.brookhavenhospital.com/depression.html

Child Trauma Academy
Houston, TX
www.ChildTrauma.org

Cleveland Clinic Health Information Center
9500 Euclid Ave, NA31
Cleveland, OH 44195
www.clevelandclinic.org
healthl@ccf.org

Depression and Bipolar Support Alliance
730 N Franklin Street
Suite 501
Chicago, IL 60610
800-826-3632
www.dbsalliance.org

Depression Screening
MayoClinic Online
www.MayoClinic.com

MOPS—Mothers of Preschoolers
MOPS International exists to encourage, equip, and develop every mother of preschoolers—urban, suburban, rural, stay-at-home, working, teen, single, and married—moms with different lifestyles who share a similar desire to be the very best moms they can be. To find or start a MOPS group and access the many resources of MOPS visit www.MOPS.org or call 1-888-910-6677.

National Institute of Mental Health
6001 Executive Blvd
Bethesda, MD 20892
www.nlm.nih.gov/medlineplus/postpartumdepression.html
www.nimh.nih.gov/publicat/numbers/cfm

National Mental Health Association
2001 N. Beauregard Street
12th Floor
Alexandria, VA 22311
800-969-6642
www.nmha.org

OBGYN.net
Timothy R. B. Johnson, MD
Barbara Apgar, MD
www.obgyn.net

PostPartum Support International
Helpline 800-944-4PPD
For support groups in your area: www.postpartum.net

Prevent Child Abuse America
200 South Michigan Ave
Chicago, IL 60604
www.PreventChildAbuse.org

Usana Health Sciences
www.usana-nutritionals.com

Q & A: The Doctor Is In

This book would not be complete without some specific information on postpartum depression (PPD). My problems were multidimensional (to say the least), but it's clear that PPD was the trigger that sent me literally over the edge.

Perhaps you are suffering from postpartum depression. It's my hope, no matter how deep your own trials have been, that you have received a large dose of hope and help in these pages, encouraging you to put one foot in front of the other. But I'm very aware that I am limited in how much I can help. I'm a survivor not a doctor. So I asked Dr. Michael O'Toole, one of the doctors who treated me *after* my depression led me to the bridge, to give some information on PPD. Please use these questions and answers as a starting place to see if your own search for emotional and physical wholeness should include more research on your part—and especially a trip to a trusted healthcare provider who can answer your questions.

What is PPD?

According to the *Diagnostic and Statistical Manual of Mental Disorders*, 4th edition (DSM-IV), PPD is medically defined by the same criteria as clinical depression, except it is a major depressive episode that presents itself within four weeks of childbirth. (Many health professionals, however, would extend this out to three months after delivery, and several studies have actually looked at a twelve-month period.) The nine symptoms are:

1. depressed mood
2. markedly diminished interest or pleasure in activities, also known as anhedonia
3. appetite disturbances (usually a loss of appetite with weight loss)
4. sleep disturbances (most often insomnia and/or fragmented sleep)
5. physical agitation or, less common, psychomotor slowing
6. fatigue or decreased energy
7. feelings of worthlessness or excessive or inappropriate guilt
8. decreased concentration or ability to make decisions
9. recurrent thoughts of death or suicidal thoughts

The definition of major depression requires five of these nine symptoms to be present, one of which must be depressed mood or anhedonia. These symptoms also have to be present most of the time, nearly every day, for at least a two-week span.

What causes PPD?

The cause of PPD is a subject of much debate. Many of the hypotheses cite a mix of biological, chemical, social, and psychological factors as the cause, and any combination of these factors can predispose or possibly cause a woman to suffer from PPD. While the exact cause is unknown, there are many factors that increase a woman's risk for developing PPD. The biggest risk is depression or anxiety during pregnancy.

Other factors that can cause or predispose a woman to PPD are hormonal changes, stressful life events, a previous history of depression, being single, cigarette smoking, and illegal drug use. A woman who has had a previous history of PPD or bipolar disorder would be considered high risk.

Women can be pulled in many directions, and this can increase their chances of becoming depressed. Today many women work outside the home and are expected to be a homemaker and the primary caregiver to the child (and the perfect wife to her husband) at the same time. Trying to blend all of these different roles can be a source of considerable frustration, particularly if the woman is the sole supporter both financially and emotionally for the child. Many times, trying to adjust to the new baby is another stressor that can be a source of depression. The woman goes from being pregnant to someone who is actually a mother and in nearly total charge of a new life. This can affect her interpersonal relationships and can cause stressors at home.

While she is pregnant a woman has an idealized fantasy of

what motherhood will be like, and then reality hits, and it can be significantly different from her ideal. A woman's excitement about being a new mother can be tempered by a sense of sadness, anger, or even the loss of a simpler life. She may even have new marital stressors now that her life is more complicated. Other life stressors can contribute to a woman's developing PPD. This is a broad category that encompasses almost all outside influences that could cause stress, such as financial difficulties, recent significant loss, or health problems in the mother or infant. Another suspected cause could be an imbalance of neurotransmitters in the brain.

Most likely the cause of depression is not any single factor but a combination of factors, and obviously no two women are the same.

How long does PPD last?

PPD can be managed effectively in a short amount of time. In many untreated cases of PPD, it is self-limiting, resolving within seven months. This can vary widely from individual to individual. When left untreated, however, PPD can have profound effects on the mother, infant, and family. But if treated appropriately, PPD can be managed effectively.

When the depression is prolonged, its severity can also increase. Of women with a history of major depression, 50 to 85 percent will have at least one more episode when they discontinue medication. This incidence increases incrementally with each number of previous episodes. Long-term treatment should be considered and would be indicated in any woman with a history of three or more major depression episodes.

How often does PPD affect women?

PPD occurs in approximately 10 to 15 percent of all pregnancies. That means approximately one out of every eight women will be affected after childbirth. PPD is the most common complication of childbearing. About 500,000 women in the United States will be affected by PPD every year.

Women who have suffered from PPD have approximately a 25 percent chance of recurrence in a subsequent pregnancy. This means that one in every four women will have a reoccurrence. One of the compounding factors that can make it difficult to tell exactly how often PPD occurs is the stigma attached to reporting depression. It is important for women to realize that PPD is not a failure on their part, or is in some way their fault, but is rather a recognized medical illness.

What can the family do?

The most important role of the family is to provide supportive care for the new mother. Many studies have shown that a strong support structure can help decrease the incidence of PPD. Another important role of the family is to bring any concerns they may have about the new mother to the attention of her healthcare provider. This will allow the mother to be more appropriately assessed, and if she has PPD, treatment can be started.

Should a "blue funk" or "baby blues" be considered a problem to be treated?

A "blue funk" or postpartum "baby blues" does not need to be treated. By definition, this condition is self-limiting and should resolve itself within a short period of time. The blues normally resolves in ten to fourteen days after delivery. Also, by definition, this condition does not hinder the new mom from performing her daily activities, so she will still be able to function adequately. The key, however, is not to miss PPD by assuming it is the blues.

While the blues often causes a new mother to have a gloomy mood, crying spells, and sad feelings, the condition does not generally affect her view of herself, including her self-esteem or feelings of self-worth, which PPD certainly can affect. In summary, postpartum "baby blues" does not need to be treated, but it remains imperative that one does not just assume a condition is the blues. Observe closely and if there is a question about it being PPD, have the condition thoroughly evaluated.

Are there predisposing factors for PPD?

Predisposing factors can include hormonal changes, stressful life events, a personal history of depression, and a family history of depression. Factors that do not appear to put a new mother at risk are her education level, the new baby's gender, breast-feeding, the type of delivery, and the fact that the pregnancy was unplanned. Also, cultures with a strong support system for new mothers often have a lower rate of PPD.

What is postpartum psychosis?

Postpartum psychosis is more severe than PPD but thankfully much more rare. Postpartum psychosis occurs following only one to two births per thousand and is most often a manifestation of bipolar disorder. Symptoms of postpartum psychosis are hallucinations, delusions, restless behavior, mania, as well as disorganization of thought and bizarre behavior. Women with a preexisting psychotic illness, especially bipolar disorder, are at the highest risk, as well as women with a prior history of PPD. Postpartum psychosis usually presents within the first two weeks after delivery and has a high risk of recurrence in the next pregnancy. Once postpartum psychosis has been identified, rapid referral to a psychiatrist is critical.

What steps can I take if I have symptoms of depression during pregnancy or after childbirth?

If a woman has any symptoms of depression, the most important first step is getting in contact with her healthcare provider so that her symptoms can be fully and adequately assessed. Treatment could range anywhere from counseling to antidepressants. After she discusses her wishes with her healthcare provider, and if medications are required, a thorough discussion is needed regarding the risks as well as benefits of medications. Immediate help to decrease some of the negative effects that can result from untreated depression—specifically the negative impact on the mother, on mother-baby bonding, and on the family—is essential.

How is PPD treated?

Before PPD can be treated, it must be identified. That is the first step. The treatment depends on the severity of the depression. Treatment can range from counseling to antidepressants to ECT (electroconvulsive therapy). If a woman is diagnosed with major depression, treatment with an antidepressant medication is appropriate. There are studies showing that antidepressants help with PPD, and there are studies showing that counseling/psychotherapy can also help.

Once again, the woman along with her healthcare provider has to decide on the appropriate course of treatment. This must be individualized from woman to woman based on her needs.

If antidepressants are considered and she is currently breast-feeding, she must decide if she will continue to breast-feed. (See the question on breast-feeding below for more information.) The most important thing is that the depression is taken care of in a timely manner and handled in such a way as to help minimize any negative effects (psychosocial effects, which affect relationships with other family members, and/or the inability to bond with the baby, thus causing negative effects on the infant). When using an antidepressant to treat PPD, it is important that, once the medicines have been initiated and tailored to therapeutic doses, the woman stay on them for a minimum of six months to help prevent relapse.

Another treatment option that can be considered when a woman suffers from severe depression is ECT. One must always consider the severity of the depression, the woman's desires, whether she has suffered from depression previously, and what treatments or medications worked previously. All of these will affect the decision to use ECT, antidepressants, or counseling/psychotherapy.

If this is the woman's third time of having a depressive episode, she should consider staying on antidepressants long term. Recurrence of depression can develop in 50 to 85 percent of women some time after medication has been stopped.

What effects can untreated depression have?

Depression often goes untreated because women minimize their symptoms for fear of the stigma that may be attached to depression, as well as the feelings of failure or inadequacy that she may have.

When a woman has a mental illness, there can be several consequences, such as stress within the family, loss of wages, and the child being removed from the home. PPD can affect a woman's ability to parent appropriately, and since some of the symptoms are lack of energy and inability to concentrate, her ability to care for her child's physical and emotional needs may be impaired. PPD can also increase a woman's level of irritability, which can make it more difficult for her to meet her child's normal need for attention. There could be missed pediatric appointments as well as increased psychiatric disturbances in the child and greater difficulty in forming attachment relationships.

Because many women suffering from PPD have an impaired ability to care for their infant, these children can have a delay in cognitive and motor development. In addition they have been shown to have more insecure attachments with their mother and with other adults when compared to children whose mothers were not depressed. They may also have gaze aversion, decreased eye contact, fewer vocalizations, delayed language development, and lower activity level, being less prone to explore their environment than other infants.

Maternal depression can also induce a depressive-type state in the infant, which in turn can cause a deeper depression in the mother. Supportive household members can try to offset these negative effects to the baby by providing the cognitive, emotional, and physical stimulation that the infant requires. Obviously this can be difficult to accomplish, because normally the mother is the infant's primary caregiver and others may not have the time, inclination, or ability to give the appropriate care.

Depression can also affect relationships with everyone else who comes in contact with the new mother, whether it is her spouse, family members, or friends. In some cases the depression leads to suicide or infanticide. Since the consequences of not treating depression can be dire, it is imperative that depression be recognized and treated appropriately.

Is the estrogen patch a good treatment for PPD?

There are studies that have looked at the effects of hormone therapy on PPD, and some show that estrogen may have a mild benefit for PPD. The use of hormones, however, would certainly have to be tempered with the known risks that are associated with estrogens, specifically the increased incidence of blood clots. This is a serious concern after childbirth, when a woman's risk of blood clots is increased.

The possibility of decreased milk production also exists when a breast-feeding mother is on estrogen. Also of note, in one of the studies regarding estrogen, even though there was some improvement, the majority of women in that study were still having depressive symptoms. Therefore it would be reasonable to conclude that estrogen should certainly not be a first-line drug of choice, if it is considered at all.

Is breast-feeding safe if I am in PPD and taking medications?

The answer to that is more complicated than it appears on the surface. Antidepressant therapy may carry a risk for infants, but as I have previously indicated, untreated depression is also risky, not only to the mother but to the baby as well. Therefore, the risks and benefits must be weighed for each woman. With the data that we have available, there are antidepressants that certainly appear relatively safe with breast-feeding (as long as one realizes that some of these drugs have not been thoroughly studied and very few have any data regarding long-term complications for the babies).

At this time, due to limitations in the data as well as the lack of long-term follow-up studies, nothing can be guaranteed to be 100 percent safe. While breast-feeding is certainly recommended from a medical standpoint, the more important thing is that the depression be taken care of. If a new mother is reluctant to take antidepressant medications because of possible effects to her baby, her depression may go unresolved. Doing nothing can certainly have a much more detrimental effect than discontinuing breast-feeding and going on antidepressant therapy.

To date, no adverse effects on breast-fed infants from some of the antidepressants have been reported. Overall when considering breast-feeding and taking medicines, it is certainly recommended that treatment be individualized to each person, using the lowest effective dose of the safest medication (while consulting with the infant's pediatrician).

How important is it to be screened for PPD?

Every woman should be screened for PPD in the postpartum period. One of the easiest times for this would be at her routine postpartum visit. It is important to evaluate every woman because depression can significantly interfere with healthy family relationships and because it can be life threatening to the woman and even her baby. Also at the routine visit it is important to assess the woman's level of support—her support system at home—and to provide family members with information while trying to involve them in any needed follow-up.

Involving family members can help the woman feel more connected, as well as help alleviate some of the helplessness that family members may feel as they watch the woman go from happy to depressed in a short period of time. When the mother goes for the PPD test (as long as it is okay with her), I recommend that the person who has been with her during the pregnancy and delivery (a husband, mother, friend) go with her. This person can help report the true extent of the depression. It's a known fact that many women tend to under-report depression. A woman may feel guilty or think that she should not be having any depressed feelings because of the idealized picture of motherhood she may have. Society says new mothers should/will always be completely happy and full of joy. If this is not the case, a woman is likely to try to hide any negative feelings. This is the reason some form of official screening to catch depression is necessary. If someone the woman trusts also hears the diagnosis, it gives the woman permission to accept her condition and move forward with the proper treatment.

Two screening methods can be used for PPD. First, there are standardized questionnaires. There are multiple varieties, but one of the most common is the EPDS (Edinburgh Postnatal Depression Scale), which is a simple questionnaire that takes only a couple of minutes to fill out. Her answers to the ten questions may trigger her healthcare provider to delve deeper, as needed, to further assess her depression.

The second screening method is when the healthcare provider asks a woman about the symptoms of depression and assesses whether her responses meet the criteria laid out by the DSM-IV (*Diagnostic and Statistical Manual of Mental Disorders,* fourth edition). Either one of these methods would be appropriate. The first one, of course, based on the written responses, could trigger the face-to-face meeting with the healthcare provider where the woman would be fully assessed.

The U.S. Preventive Service Task Force recommends that all

adults be screened for depression, and they suggest screening with a simple two-question tool:

1. Over the past two weeks have you felt down, depressed, or hopeless?
2. Over the past two weeks have you felt little interest or pleasure in doing things?

If the answer to either of these is yes, a complete evaluation is indicated.

Dr. Michael O'Toole did his undergraduate studies at the University of Alabama at Birmingham where he received his B.S. in biology. He then went on to medical school at University of South Alabama College of Medicine and did his residency in obstetrics and gynecology at St. John's Mercy Medical Center in St. Louis. Currently Dr. O'Toole is in full-time private practice. He lives with his wife and their four children in Green Bay, Wisconsin.